WOMEN IN THE
Wild Blue

Target-Towing WASP at Camp Davis

David A. Stallman

Women Airforce Service Pilots In WWII

WOMEN IN THE
Wild Blue

Target-Towing WASP at Camp Davis

David A. Stallman

ISBN 0-9708239-3-2

Manufactured in the United States of America

Printed by:

Carlisle Printing
OF WALNUT CREEK Ltd.

2673 TR 421
Sugarcreek, OH 44681

Dedication…

To my wife and best friend Carol—
thank you for your hours of reading,
consultation and encouragement, all
of which helped make this a reality.

Contents

Part I – WASP Beginnings

Part II – WASP At Camp Davis

Part III – WASP Then and Now

Acknowledgments

I AM INDEBTED to the many WASP and their families who contributed their thoughts, interviews, pictures and encouragement. They want their story told. I am especially grateful for my personal relationships with Helen Wyatt Snapp and Frances Rohrer Sargent. These women guided and encouraged me with many conversations. Meeting them and others at WASP Fly-Ins in Lakeland, Florida and Sweetwater, Texas in 2005 was invaluable to my work. Their stories were so compelling that I committed to thorough research to capture the "real" Camp Davis WASP history and publish it before all these wonderful women are gone.

I also want to thank the people at Texas Woman's University— TWU, the National Archive for WASP in Denton, Texas. The TWU Library contains the official WASP records and as such, provides an official source of WASP information. They were most helpful, giving me both time and support in finding information. In particular I would like to thank Tracey MacGowan, Archivist, for her patient assistance and willingness to dig for yet another bit of information each time I called.

Finally, I thank my sister Jean for her help in the final reading of the manuscript.

Prologue

WE DO NOT pay enough tribute to the men and women who joined the WWII effort, who did behind the scenes work that supported and insured the success of our troops. One such group is the WASP – Women Airforce Service Pilots.

When I wrote *ECHOES of Topsail – Stories of the Island's Past*, I discovered some information about the WASP stationed at Camp Davis during WWII and devoted several pages to their history. Since then, my curiosity has taken me deeper into WASP history and I have been astounded by what these young women did. They broke from traditional roles that branded women as housewives, secretaries, hairdressers and teachers, to name a few. They had the will and determination to pursue their dreams. For many WASP their heroine and inspiration was Amelia Earhart, an early pioneer in aviation who became world famous for her exploits. Their passion was flying and they each found a way to fly. I decided that these extraordinary women must be sought out and their story told.

The Camp Davis WASP story is about breaking new ground. Young women were flying pursuits, Helldivers, and bombers over long beaches, towing targets for antiaircraft gunnery recruits to fire live ammunition at. One of their projects became the genesis for radio-controlled unmanned flight. As these assignments proved successful, they were implemented at other air bases.

The heart of this story is told through Betty Deuser Budde's letters and Laurine Nielsen's logs which take you with them as they pursue their aerial dreams. Other Camp Davis WASP add their recollections to give us their perspectives. Listening to aging aviatrixes I became infatuated with their sparkling personalities as they recalled their adventures and talked about their continued dedication to WASP.

These recollections, many of them in the WASP' own words, describe what it was like for a girl just out of high school in the late 1930s, to learn to fly powerful military planes and become targets for antiaircraft artillery shells. These young women served our nation heroically in perilous times as war was raging on the European and Japanese fronts.

The WASP story tells itself as you follow their descriptions of daily routine, and of moments of fear and joy. What comes through is the determination of these young women to follow their passion and to succeed. They believed that even more than individual fulfillment, they were making a positive case for women as military pilots, realizing that it could open doors for women in the future. They were the WASP – Women Airforce Service Pilots.*

* Note that WASP is plural...Women Airforce Service Pilots.

*M*any of us married during the war, and a number of us continued flying for our livelihood. But we could never go back to the way we were. The WASP experience changed us all forever.

– Anne Noggle –

Overview

IN 1941 GENERAL "Hap" Arnold, Commanding General of the Army Air Force in Washington, DC, had tremendous challenges. The United States' war effort had a lot of catching up to do. We had declared war on Japan when they attacked Pearl Harbor and soon after, on Germany and Italy. The U.S. began issuing war bonds and stamps to help finance the war effort and we were gearing up war production. We had to prepare to wage war on two hemispheres, at sea, in the air and on the ground.

General Arnold began a reorganization plan to modernize the U.S. air arsenal. It was said in 1940 that of the 800 planes in the U.S. arsenal, 700 were obsolete. Airplane production rose at unprecedented levels. We produced 19,000 in 1941; 48,000 in 1942; 86,000 in 1943 and 96,000 in 1944. With that as a backdrop, you can see why pilot training, mechanics, and ferrying of airplanes would need manpower.

Two women played key roles in the search for a solution to the Air Force's problem, both arguing against the instincts of General Arnold, who was not convinced women had a piloting role to play in the war effort.

Jacqueline Cochran was committed to bringing women pilots into the Air Force on a broad scale. She was a world-renowned aviatrix who held racing titles including first in the women's division of the Bendix Cross Country event and third place against a field of men pilots, and she was a bright and determined woman.

Since her first contact with Eleanor Roosevelt in 1939, Jacqueline Cochran had been trying to sell her idea of bringing women into the Air Force to ferry airplanes.

Another famous aviatrix, Nancy Harkness Love, also had a role in finding a solution to the Air Force's manpower problem. Love, too, had impressive credentials and flying records. She was already working as a civilian in the Air Transport Command Ferrying Division office in Baltimore, Maryland. She proposed to assemble a group of commercial level female pilots with 500 logged hours, who would require just a few weeks of training in order to fly military planes. They were to ferry planes from factory to airbases thus relieving male pilots for combat duty. Her idea was explored and the program approved, however, she was able only to muster 28 experienced candidates.

Jackie Cochran, after a stint in England to help that country organize its women flyers, returned to an already organized Women's Auxiliary Ferrying Squadron, WAFS, headed by Nancy Love, that was beginning to ferry light aircraft from factories to air bases. Cochran was enraged that Love's plan had been approved and implemented.

Sometime in 1942 General Arnold, recognizing the need for a bigger program and broader women's involvement, agreed to a new plan submitted by Jackie Cochran. General Arnold could see that a program of this scale was essential because of the increasingly severe shortage of pilots.

Jackie proposed that the Air Force should bring in women with private licenses and only 35 logged hours of flying time…fewer credentials than Love's women, but, nonetheless, very capable pilots. She was able to find 1830 women who qualified. The women's qualification minimums were set at age 18, and 5 ft 2 1/2 inches in height. Their basic pilot training would take seven months.

So Cochran's program was put into effect and the women pilots' training began in Houston, Texas, later moving to Avenger Field at Sweetwater, Texas. The training organization was named Women Flying Training Detachment – WFTD. In August, 1943 the Women's Auxiliary Ferrying Squadron – WAFS and WFTD were merged and renamed Women Airforce Service Pilots – WASP. Jackie Cochran was appointed Director of Woman Pilots – AAF, and Nancy Love served as Executive Director on the ATC Ferrying Division staff. They had offices in different cities and stayed clear of each other. But Love apparently accepted her position and worked well in it with little involvement with Cochran, her director.

At some point in the reorganization the military wanted Cochran to attach to the Women Army Corp – WAC that was headed by highly recognized and capable Colonel Oveta Culp Hobby. But a determined Jackie declared: *I will not serve under a woman who doesn't know her...from a propeller.* It seems clear that Jackie feared that she and her WASP would disappear in the WAC organization.

Of the 1830 women who entered the program, 1074 ultimately earned their wings. This "wash-out" rate was comparable to that of the male pilots' training results. Cochran expected the women pilots to receive the same rigorous training as their male counterparts. They were to be instructed in all the various aspects of flight and navigation skills.

These women were civil servants, but required to follow military regimens. Because of the natural attraction between men and women, and because of the unique role they were playing, Cochran imposed a lot of restrictions to insure that her WASP stayed on task. Sweetwater was dubbed "Cochran's Convent."

Class 43-3 received their wings in July, 1943 and twenty-five of them reported to Camp Davis for their first assignment and further training. Their acceptance was less than enthusiastic...in fact, downright hostile by some. The male pilots saw the women as a threat and, after all, if replaced it would mean they would have to go into combat. It is said that Camp Davis Commander Colonel Stephenson was not at all happy about his new responsibility for these women. He no doubt saw them as a problem he didn't want to have.

A month later, the second group of twenty-five, Class 43-4, received their wings and reported to Camp Davis. Two additional WASP came in to replace two who had lost their lives. This brought the total WASP count to 52 at Camp Davis. Throughout the war other air bases typically had 8 to 12 WASP. [In the first two months at Camp Davis two WASP died in plane crashes and a third was injured. This had a profound impact on the WASP pilots, but most of them accepted the risks and tried to learn from the crashes. There were some claims of sabotage, but basically they were working with planes that required a lot of maintenance since the new ones went for combat. Their fatality rate was no higher than the male pilots.]

Jackie Cochran continually visited her women at Camp Davis, insisting each time that their training include the biggest planes and that they be assigned target-towing work. She made demands that resulted in their flying larger planes like pursuits, the A-24 and A-25, B-34, and towing targets, important moments in the evolution of this new role for women pilots. In the early months the WASP program was a tightly held experiment that was not released to the public because the war department needed to see if it would be successful.

Camp Davis was the original base for another secret program, that of training pilots to fly radio-controlled drone planes. 15 WASP were part of that secret program. They received initial training at Camp Davis then transferred to Liberty Field, Georgia. From there, after more training, they dispersed to other locations to do radio-control drone flying and to train others.

In March, 1944 antiaircraft artillery training was winding down at Camp Davis. The rest of the WASP transferred to Liberty Field,

Georgia, and to other locations. Assignments were varied, with most of the women continuing in the radio-controlled drone program and the rest carrying on target-towing and strafing missions at bases throughout the country until the WASP program was finally concluded in December, 1944.

For many reasons, the WASP were organized as civil servants working under military rules. There were a number of efforts to grant WASP military status, but they failed until it was successfully signed into law in 1977...33 years later.

In the end, the WASP flew over 60 million miles in 78 different types of aircraft. Each WASP typically was qualified on 10 to 12 aircraft; no small feat for a group of women whose abilities and stamina were doubted by most at the outset. They earned the respect of many and a place in history.

Timeline

3.1939	Jacqueline Cochran sends letter to Eleanor Roosevelt suggesting that women could serve as military pilots.
6.1940	General Henry "Hap" Arnold rejects Love's plan for experienced women pilots.
9.1940	U.S. Air strength shockingly inadequate – 700 of 800 planes obsolete.
10.1940	General Hap Arnold named Deputy Chief of Staff, Army Air Force.
10.1940	Germany wreaks heavy raids on London – London "Blitz." Winston Churchill's "Blood, Toil, Tears" speech.
11.1940	Franklin D. Roosevelt re-elected President for a third term.
4.1941	First troops arrive at newly constructed Camp Davis.
6.1941	Cochran first woman to fly a military aircraft across Atlantic.
7.1941	President and Mrs. Roosevelt lunch with Cochran – supportive of women pilots.
12.1941	Civil Air Patrol established to train civilian pilots.

12.1941	Pearl Harbor attacked by Japanese – U.S. declares war on Japan.
12.1941	Germany and Italy declare war on the U.S. and U.S. declares war.
12.1941	Airplane production increased to 19,000.
9.1942	Women's Auxiliary Ferrying Squadron WAFS – organized and headed by Nancy Love.
9.1942	Women's Flying Training Detachment WFTD – organized and headed by Jacqueline Cochran.
11.1942	28 prospective WASP report to Houston for training.
12.1942	Airplane production rose to 48,000.
4.1943	WASP training move from Houston to Avenger Field completed.
7.1943	First 25 WASP report to Camp Davis.
8.1943	Mabel Rawlinson – first Camp Davis WASP to die in plane crash.
8.1943	Second group of 25 WASP report to Camp Davis.
8.1943	WAFS & WFTD merge to become WASP – Women Airforce Service Pilots.
9.1943	Betty Taylor Wood – second Camp Davis WASP to die in plane crash.
9.1943	Italy's unconditional surrender to General Eisenhower.
10.1943	15 Camp Davis WASP to Liberty Field, Georgia for radio-controlled target drone training.
12.1943	Airplane production now at 86,000 for the year.

2.1944	WASP finally get their Santiago Blue uniforms.
4.1944	Balance of Camp Davis WASP transferred to Liberty Field, Georgia.
6.1944	D Day – Normandy invasion.
11.1944	Franklin D. Roosevelt re-elected for his fourth term as President – Harry Truman as Vice President.
12.1944	Women Airforce Service Pilots Deactivated – Attempts to militarize WASP failed.
3.1945	Hitler commits suicide.
5.1945	VE Day – Victory in Europe.
8.1945	Bombing of Hiroshima and Nagasaki.
8.1945	VJ Day – Japan surrenders.
11.1977	President Jimmy Carter signs legislation providing military status and benefits for WASP.

PART ONE

WASP Beginnings

AVIATION ENTERPRISES LTD.

General Henry "Hap" Arnold
1886 - 1950

HENRY ARNOLD WAS born in Gladwyn, Pennsylvania on June 25, 1886. Following graduation from the United States Military Academy he was appointed a Second Lieutenant of Infantry on June 14, 1907. In 1911 he entered aviation and became a flyer. After completing training, he was detailed to the Signal Corps in April, and began piloting the Wright bi-plane. He was one of the first flyers taught by the Wright Brothers.

TWU General Henry "Hap" Arnold

In June, 1912 Arnold, known as Hap, established a new altitude record when he piloted a Brugree-Wright airplane to a height of 6,540 feet. He progressed rapidly through military ranks and by February, 1935 he had received the temporary rank of Brigadier General. On September 29, 1938 he was named Chief of Staff of the Air Corps.

With Hitler's growing war machine, Arnold became concerned

about America's lack of combat aircraft. He discussed U.S. air power vs German air power with President Roosevelt, and the decision was made to build 11,000 new combat aircraft. General Arnold commanded that civilian flying schools be established to train Air Corps pilots to fly the new planes. Then in 1941 the Army Air Forces was established and Major General Arnold became Chief of Staff for Air and Chief of the Army Air Forces.

During the early months of 1942 General Arnold, encountering a severe shortage of male pilots due to heavy losses of combat pilots, approved a plan submitted by Jacqueline Cochran to train young women pilots to fly military aircraft within the U.S. This would relieve male pilots for combat duty. An earlier approved plan initiated by Nancy Love had proved inadequate. On September 14, 1942 the Women's Flying Training Detachment was established at the Houston Municipal Airport, with Jacqueline Cochran as its Director. Three months later General Arnold approved moving the training program to Avenger Field in Sweetwater, Texas. After training there, the women were transferred to Camp Davis in North Carolina.

At Camp Davis these women pilots quickly filled a need in the programs for ferrying planes and for target towing in antiaircraft artillery practice. But living conditions were rough and they had to make do with men's military issue, a source of many humorous moments in daily life on the base. Finally, in May of 1943, General Hap Arnold authorized Jacqueline Cochran to oversee the design of a suitable uniform for the women pilots. He wanted it to be blue. In concurrence with the announcement of the new Santiago Blue uniforms, on August 20th General Arnold issued orders: "The acronym for all AAF women pilots will be WASP – Women Airforce Service Pilots." The women finally got official recognition. Then in March the following year they were issued their own uniforms. Full military status, however, was not to be conferred until much later.

General Arnold retired from the service on June 30, 1946 with the ratings of Command Pilot and Combat Observer. His many accomplishments of both personal and national significance gained him the distinction of becoming the first five-star General of the United States Air Force on May 7, 1949 by an act of Congress. He died on January 15, 1950 of a cardiac condition.

No one could put it better than WASP Deanie Parrish in her tribute:
> Let not there be any doubt of the WASP' pride in General Henry Hap Arnold, the man who, among his many accomplishments, authorized the creation and naming of the WASP – a man who had the imagination to see success and the confidence to create it.

Source: *Wings Across America* by WASP, Deanie Parrish

Jacqueline Cochran
1910-1980

JACQUELINE COCHRAN WAS born in Florida in 1910 and orphaned soon after. She grew up with a poor family and had very little formal education, but was gifted with a drive to succeed. In her teen and later years she aggressively pursued a career in cosmetics, and went to the top of her profession as the owner of a prestigious salon and a developer of a line of cosmetics. Her husband-to-be, millionaire businessman Floyd Odlum, suggested that she learn to fly in order to be more effective in her use of sales time and travel.

TWU Jacqueline Cochran

She agreed and who could know how it would change her life. Cochran mastered flying in a few weeks and soon owned her first airplane, a Travelair, later graduating to a Northrop Gamma. She became deeply committed to flying yet she found a way to keep her cosmetics business going all through the war into the 1950s.

Cochran became a test pilot and a world renowned aviatrix. Among her early accomplishments she tested the first turbo-supercharger ever installed on an aircraft engine in 1934. Her taste for record setting was keen; she was the first woman to fly a bomber across the Atlantic Ocean. She held racing titles including first in the women's division of the Bendix Cross Country event and third place against a field of men pilots. Jackie Cochran was clearly a bright and determined woman.

While pursuing her flying passion, Cochran saw a way to promote her idea that women pilots could ferry new military airplanes from factories to air bases, freeing male pilots for other duties. She discussed it with Eleanor Roosevelt in 1939 and found her very accepting, as Eleanor always promoted the advancement of women. Some time later she approached General Hap Arnold with her idea. General Arnold thought it had possibilities but wasn't convinced, so Jackie gathered information about women licensed pilots along with their flying hours. Getting little support for her plan from the U.S. Air Force but a warmer reception from the Royal Air Force, she traveled to England to help the RAF set up a women pilots group for ferrying military aircraft.

Upon returning to the U.S. she found that Nancy Love had been

TWU Jackie Cochran

approved to set up a similar plan using 28 experienced, commercial level female pilots, named Women Auxiliary Flying Squadron. Jackie went to Arnold demanding an explanation and again arguing her broader plan, finally coming away with her own approved program in September, 1942, named Women's Flying Training Detachment. In August, 1943 the WAFS and WFTD were merged and renamed Women Airforce Service Pilots - WASP. Cochran was named Director of Women Pilots - AAF, and Nancy Love became Executive Director on the

ATC Ferrying Division staff.

By early 1944 air superiority had been achieved in Europe and American pilots began to come home to few piloting jobs. It was apparent that the WASP program was nearing its end as well. Cochran's women pilots had made their mark and acquitted themselves well. Jackie had one final desire; she wanted the WASP to be militarized in order to discharge them with military veteran status, and for this she saw no compromise. She compiled an exhaustive report detailing the WASP accomplishments and released it to the press. Cochran insisted that General Arnold find a way to militarize her program including pilot training under her command. Her wish was not to be fulfilled just then. General Arnold de-activated WASP December 20, 1944, acknowledging the women had exceeded all expectations, but refusing to broach the idea of military status.

Jackie Cochran remained at the Pentagon as a special consultant to General Hap Arnold and was awarded the Distinguished Service Medal for her wartime service. In 1948 she finally received her military commission – Lieutenant Colonel in the U. S. Air Force Reserves. Continuing to establish new speed records, she became the first woman to break the sound barrier in 1953.

Jacqueline Cochran died in 1980 at her ranch in Indio, California. In 1996, the United States Postal Service honored Jacqueline Cochran with the airmail postage stamp.

Nancy Harkness Love
1914 - 1976

NANCY HARKNESS WAS born on February 14, 1914 in Houghton, Michigan. She developed an intense interest in aviation at an early age. Sixteen years old in 1930, she took her first flight and earned her pilot's license within a month. Later, she would carry this love of flying with her to Vassar College in Poughkeepsie, New York, where it is said that she was restless and adventurous. She earned extra money by renting a plane and taking fellow students for rides. One time she flew low over campus, almost touching the treetops, and someone turned in her plane's tail numbers. University officials were not amused. She was suspended from school for two weeks and forbidden to fly for the rest of the semester.

HWS Nancy Harkness Love

Leaving her college studies, Nancy continued to pursue her flying career. She was a charter member of the Ninety-Nines, a female pilots' organization founded by Amelia Earhart. In 1935 she was one of several women hired by the Bureau of Air Commerce to work on its Air Marking Program, a Works Projects Administration program to mark water towers, barn roofs, and the like, with city names and compass headings as aids to air navigation.

By 1936 Nancy and her husband Robert Love were running their own business, Inter City Aviation, out of Boston Airport. In 1937 and 1938 she flew as a test pilot for Gwinn Air Car Company, performing safety tests on various aircraft modifications including the new tricycle landing gear that would be adopted on large aircraft. She was one of several Massachusetts women who ferried light planes to the Canadian border. It was during these ferry flights that she made her first contacts with the Army Air Corps' Air Ferrying Command.

In 1942, after the outbreak of World War II, Nancy Love accompanied her husband to Washington, DC where he was to serve active duty. She soon landed a civilian post with the Air Transport Command (ATC) Ferrying Division operation office in Baltimore, Maryland. She continued to add to her 1,200-plus flying hours by piloting her own airplane on her daily commute from the couple's home in Washington. Even prior to her move to Washington she had recognized the potential for women ferrying pilots. She succeeded in convincing the head of the Ferrying Division's Domestic Wing, then Colonel William H. Tunner, that using experienced women pilots to supplement the existing pilot force was a good idea.

She envisioned the use of a small number of exceptionally well qualified women pilots who would need only a minimum of training to transition to military aircraft. Some 28 candidates qualified, holding commercial pilot rating, but they were in short supply.

With Colonel Tunner's support the Women's Auxiliary Ferrying Squadron -WAFS was established in September, 1942 and began operations at New Castle Army Airfield, Wilmington, Delaware under ATC's 2d Ferrying Group. With only four to six weeks of transitional training to acquaint them with military procedure, they performed ferry duty for the Air Transport Command.

HWS Nancy Love

In 1943, the WAFS and the Women's Flying Training Detachment - WFTD merged and became a single entity known as the Women's Airforce Service Pilots - WASP, with Nancy Love serving as executive director on the ATC Ferrying Division staff, reporting to Jacqueline Cochran, Director of Women Pilots – AAF. Nancy was a hands-on manager and often delivered aircraft herself. Her duties included administration of six WASP ferrying squadrons and planning operational and training procedures. Charged with transporting military aircraft between factories, modification centers, depots and operational units, this highly experienced group of aviatrixes freed male pilots for combat duty. Under Love's leadership her squadrons amassed remarkable records of achievement.

Nancy Love's personal contributions included some equally remarkable achievements. She was proficient in C-47s, A-36s and fourteen other types of military aircraft. She was the first woman in U. S. military history to fly the B-25, flying it coast-to-coast in record time, and, accompanied by Betty Gillies, was one of the first two women to check out in a B-17. At the end of the war she and her husband had the unique distinction of being simultaneously awarded the Air Medal for their leadership and service in World War II.

After the war Nancy Love continued as an aviation industry leader and was a promoter for recognition of the women who had served as WASP as military veterans. They received veteran's status in 1977 shortly after her death on October 22, 1976.

Houston

JACQUELINE COCHRAN'S PROGRAM got off to a shaky start. WASP training started in November, 1942 in Houston, Texas. Civilian contractors from an air school near Houston were the instructors and the municipal airport was used for their flight work. The women who signed on lived in tourist camp cottages scattered throughout Houston and they were transported to the fields by bus. A couple of student letters and journal entries by Betty Deuser, Laurine Nielsen, and Lois Brooks give us some personal comments about their experience.

January 23, 1943, Student Betty Deuser wrote one of her many letters home: Guess what? I soloed today. Yep…and as far as I know it's first solo of our class. I'd better not feel too good, though, cuz then I'll do worse tomorrow. Didn't solo from Municipal Airport yet, but from Dodo Field, a dirt field full of mud puddles and bushes with PTs, airliners, and bombers for sky mates. It sure keeps a guy jumping.

This is the first time I didn't enjoy any meal here and who can blame me. Boiled beef tongue and collards, I think they called it. Just another name for weeds. It was awful. And every time I took a bite of tongue I kept picturing a cow with its ugly sticky tongue curled around a hunk of hay.

February 17, 1943, Student Laurine "Rene" Nielsen entered in her journal: New instructor Mr. Palmer. He's swell. Elsie has him too and Bea. We did spins, stalls, which stunk, eights and S's, and forced landings. Three landings at Dodo where I took off with flaps down. Cut into pattern screwy at home. Cut too far down. Downwind leg. Ship is a dream. Hope I can fly it properly soon.

February 22, 1943, Betty wrote again: I had the thrill of my life today...hanging upside down 4000 ft. above Texas. I was supposed to follow through on recovery from inverted flight, but I was so scared I hung on to anything I could grab. The instructor warned me to tighten my safety belt, so I made it so tight my eyes bulged; but gosh, it's sure awful to feel like you're falling out even though its safe as anything cuz I couldn't possibly fall out even if I let go with my hands. It was so funny; my feet even left the floor and hung in mid-air. What a queer feeling. All the dirt from the plane hit my face like rocks. We must've been upside down for about 30 seconds but felt more lie 10 minutes.

Got into town with Virginia Crinklaw last night to see "Random Harvest." Gee, it was keen. We walked home from the bus line by the light of the full Texan Moon. It sure was beautiful. Both of us were wishin' – well, you know.

Because of the increasing airport traffic and poor flying conditions at Houston, the Central Flying Training Command searched for a better training location. Avenger Field at Sweetwater, Texas was selected. An existing air school for male pilots was already located there, and plans formed to move the WFTD training classes to Avenger. Classes 43.2, 43.3 and 43.4 had all entered training at Houston and transferred to Avenger by April 1943, overlapping the last male pilot class by two weeks.

Lois Brooks recalled: The rumor was that our training would move to Sweetwater, Texas and it came true. Since some WASP had soloed and completed cross country flying, they were qualified to fly their PT-19 trainers to Sweetwater. A later group flew some 20 airplanes with two girls each, to Sweetwater. The rest went by public transportation.

At Sweetwater we were pressed to make up for lost time so we could graduate and there was no time for foolishness. I didn't help it by misguiding a cross country exercise when I couldn't get my intercom to work. Tom Baker couldn't communicate with me and I was the leader who took our group of 4 BTs off course. So we had additional time to make up. I must add that I was fortunate to have Tom Baker as instructor and we remained in touch for many years.

Source: wwii-women-pilots.org by Andy Hailey

Avenger Field

Arriving at Sweetwater, Texas

HELEN SNAPP TELLS of how she got to Sweetwater in 1943. Helen left the Washington, DC area via train and arrived at Sweetwater, a hot and dusty place. She had never been away from home before. She asked a taxi driver to take her to a "reasonably priced" hotel. The hotel was a rather scary place with dim corridors and the bathroom down the hall. The next morning however, she met

HWS Avenger Field Gate

HWS Avenger Field Barracks

HWS Avenger Field Control Tower

HWS Avenger Field

another WASP-to-be and they decided to strike out for another better place, the Blue Bonnet Hotel. At the Blue Bonnet she was overwhelmed by all the chattering young women in the lobby, and thought: *What am I doing here?* But the Blue Bonnet was a nice hotel temporarily housing the women pilots, and before long they were quartered at Avenger Field. Helen said: *While we were in town the "mass transit" was a big semi-trailer-sized cattle hauler with high, tiny windows. That was to become our transportation from Avenger to other flying fields and to town. With time the trailer was improved with the addition of seats.*

Avenger Field

Situated about 40 miles west of Abilene, Sweetwater, Texas was a bleak and arid place on a windy hill, known for its sweltering summers, remoteness, and snakes. Temperatures reached 100 degrees and stayed there until fall. When dust storms blew in the WASP

HWS Canteen Pause

would wrap scarves over their noses and mouths to go out and hold the planes down. Even though they were tied down, the airplanes were in danger of being blown loose from their moorings. It was a challenge to keep their barracks clean and acceptable for inspection. It meant ongoing efforts to get rid of the grit that kept blowing in.

Accommodations

The women's barracks were laid out 6 WASP to a room with one bathroom between two rooms of 12 women. They marched everywhere they went in military style, did calisthenics, and ended their 16-hour day with taps. They were ladies with a purpose, and thus took part in parades, infantry drills, barracks inspection, and the oath of allegiance, as did the male cadets.

Avenger Field was solely dedicated to WASP training, and it

was known as "Cochran's Convent." She forbade any relationships with instructors or other men, especially cadets from other airfields. They did have occasional dances where other cadets were invited for the evening, nothing else. The WASP stayed in line because they were told they would be dismissed if they violated the rules. And they would let nothing jeopardize their flying. The rules stipulated that the only time men and women could be together was during "mess," that is, during meals.

HWS Avenger Trainee

HWS Avenger Field Rest and Relaxation

Male pilots, served notice that Avenger was off limits, now and then seemed to mysteriously have engine trouble forcing them to land at Avenger...but forewarned WASP valued their new roles and preserved their convent status.

Zoot Suits

In training the women were issued oversized men's coveralls that they called "zoot suits" because of the poor

HWS Avenger Fun Moment

fit. They wore tan pants with white shirts for dress until they finally received official WASP Santiago Blue uniforms in March, 1944, the only blue uniform worn in WWII.

Win Wood's book *We Were WASP* describes how Caro Bayley came parading out to model the latest style of flight uniform for our benefit. Caro was a not-quite-five-foot-three bit of "boy bait," and the zoot suit she had acquired was size 44. Rolling up the sleeves and the legs had not helped. She was told she had to wait three weeks until a class graduated to get a recycled pair closer to her size.

HWS WASP Trainee Zoot Suits

Training

Training so many pilots was a big operation in order to provide flight hours needed. There was an endless lineup of trainer craft. When classes began at Avenger, there were 90 aircraft available. Soon after that they consistently had over 200 aircraft available. In order to accommodate the many training flights, other airstrips were used as alternatives to Avenger.

Helen Snapp comments: Early in our training we did a lot of takeoffs and landings. It was important for us to be prepared for this most critical part of flying. As part of it we practiced landing in a crosswind. When you land in a crosswind you can't just land on the three wheels normally, you put down

HWS Avenger Field Trainers

the wheel in the wind then set the other one down. Once that is learned you have confidence in about any windy condition. I loved to do the "wheel landings."

Dora Dougherty said: The army way of flying was different than the civilian way. The stall sequences were different and there were different maneuvers and ways military aircraft react than do civilian aircraft.

So even coming in with a pilot's license didn't mean the women were ready to fly military aircraft. Their training was sometimes claimed to be too aggressive. The instructors took these girls through aerobatic maneuvers, spins and loops that could be considered frivolous. But they were deemed necessary to having total control over their plane.

June 18, 1943, Betty Deuser wrote: I've learned to play part of "Old Black Joe" and "Home Sweet Home" on Lois Brooks' harmonica. Sure wish I could play well. It's fun. We are having a thunderstorm tonight - still no flying. I got in 1:14 of Link today, otherwise spent the rest of the day playing ping pong and fooling around. No gambling allowed so no poker.

DAS Stearman PT-13

HWS Avenger Toughen Bodies

And there are no walks between barracks so we have to take our shoes off when we come into our bays. Tomorrow it'll be awful after this rain. Gee whiz we'll never get out of here if we can't fly.

June 21, 1943, Betty again: Two BTs just buzzed the barracks flying real close formation and just getting over the telephone wires. Lots of planes buzz the courts here probably just to see the girls run out. Cuz we always do just to see who it is.

Did I tell you I finished the AT-6 and am now on AT-17s? Last week I finished my AT-6 night flying. Just had two hours in that and it was such a bright moonlight it was easy as flying in the daytime. But coming into the pattern was as bad as 14th and Broadway with the busses.

June 26, 1943, Laurine Nielsen journal entry: Solo cross-country with Dougherty – Big Springs, Lubbock, Spurr, and SH2O. 289 miles. Average of 138 mph. From Lubbock to Spurr at 200 mph!

Same day solo cross-country with Elsie…our last ride in a 17 together. We covered the hills around Abilene thoroughly. Saw Cox's Ranch, buzzed Lake Abilene. Did chandelles and lazy 8s. Fun!

[Chandelle is an abrupt climbing turn that begins with a dive to gain speed and uses the momentum of the plane. It is considered an advanced maneuver.]

Win Wood described in *We Were WASP*: One big problem during flight period was trying to find the auxiliary field when we were ready to land, and on finding it, to enter the traffic pattern properly. No matter how close we came to the field, I never could spot it. After one hour of gyration and concentration, I would be totally lost. All the fields below looked exactly the same.

Martha Lawson recalled: Cochran pushed us hard, but she was fair. She used to tell us over and over, you don't make any mistakes or it goes against the whole organization. And mistakes were not going to be made by this new recruit.

Flight Training

The Curriculum and Flight Training consisted of four general areas:

1. Academic instruction in technical subjects required in the ferrying of aircraft,

2. Instruction in the fundamental principles required to pilot training type aircraft,

3. Training in accepted procedures of the Air Transport Command,

4. Physical training to maintain and improve physical and mental alertness.

The training of the 1074 young women pilots was rigorous, as Cochran insisted that they have the same training as male pilots. The requirements were to include the same flight training, ground instruction, Morse code, high altitude flying, instrument training and calisthenics to toughen their bodies. For the women this meant seven months of concentrated effort, learning the rudiments of flying a broad range of aircraft. The first military planes they worked with were the PT-19 – 175 HP, and then the BT-13 – 450 HP, dubbed the "Vultee Vibrator," so named because it had a tendency to shake violently as it approached stall speed. Next came the AT-6 – 650

DAS PT-19 Trainer

HWS WASP Trainees

DAS AT-6 Advanced Trainer

DAS BT-13 Vultee

HWS Avenger Field Students

HWS Avenger Field Ground School

HP. This basic training laid the groundwork for later advancement at other fields in flying larger aircraft.

Ann Russell Darr, Class 44.3, wrote an article describing their training: From reveille to taps we practiced in ground school and the flight line and the exercise field. The 400 hours of ground school was comparable to a degree in aeronautics. We had hands-on experience with engines, communications, theory of flight, weather, lifesaving and history of aviation. We did daily calisthenics and practiced flying in a Link Trainer.

We practiced parachute landings. We trained by running as fast as we could and throwing ourselves onto the ground, Learning to land on our backs instead of breaking the fall with hand or foot and risk breaking an arm or leg. Later we jumped from a high platform, or swung down on a pulley apparatus, all in preparation for an accident.

Source: *The Women Who Flew – but Kept Silent* by Ann Darr

Link Trainer

There are some references to the Link Trainer by WASP who were in pilot training. Used heavily at Avenger Field in their earlier training, this ingenious device was also available for practice throughout their time at Camp Davis. The cockpit unit was mounted on a pedestal and the student pilot would fly by actually simulating turns, climbs and descents of a real aircraft. It also taught them the basics of instrument flying in bad weather or at night.

"Flying" the Link was a dark and hot chore, especially in the summer months, because the pilot was closed in the claustrophobic cockpit with only gages and instruments to use. This method of training was very successful as it was effective, more economical than using an aircraft, and safe since crashes could be simulated.

The instructor outside the Link could simulate rough weather conditions and send radio signals the student heard through earphones, and the student would manipulate the controls in response. The pilot flew the Link through various maneuvers and the course was traced in red ink by marking a remote map. The map would later be studied to determine how the pilot did.

HWS Link Trainer

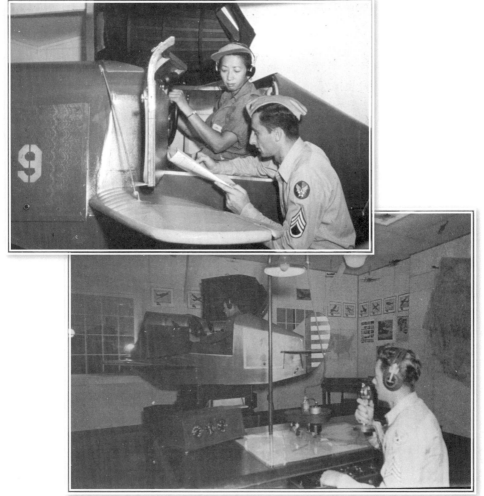

HWS Avenger Link Trainer

A Letter from Win Wood

I believe Win Wood's letter that follows is a great help to knowing what it was like first-hand. It allows us to see their early experience at Avenger through her eyes:

June, 1943

Ready Room

Dear Nina,

While waiting to go up I shall endeavor to tell you what every young girl should know about "Army life as I see it."

You will probably be very surprised to know that I have grown tremendously since joining up. At least the Army thinks so. They issued me a size 44 zoot suit. These zoot suits are GI coveralls that make even the most glamorous ones look like Dirty Gertie from Bizerte. Nothing makes them fit. I should know, I'm a walking pin cushion.

HWS Avenger Field Grads Ring Firebell

In these horrible things we fly, eat, drill, attend ground school, scrub barracks, etc. I expect orders any day that they be used as sleeping garments. We have two, laundry is very

HWS Marching Formation

hard to get and after two days they stand alone. You can imagine our plight.

The second day we were here, graduation ceremonies were held. Never have I felt so like an orphan. All the rest of the classes passed in review in their dress uniforms. Our class, who couldn't drill in our zoot suits, was put to work parking cars. By the time the fifth person expressed their amazement at my being a "real mechanic," I accepted my fate. From then on I nonchalantly said: *Oh, yes we work on the planes. Really interesting work, too.*

We had formal inspection the third day we were here. We live in bays, 6 to a bay, with shower, basin & Johnny. Two tables nailed to the wall, one bed & locker to each girl, six chairs and one wastebasket. That is the extent of our furniture. Everything has to be in a certain place, corners squared, no dust – on & on. Well, we put in three hours of hard work, scrubbing, dusting, every nook & cranny. Here comes the Lieutenant. We snap to attention by our beds. He walks in. Everything was beautiful, 100%. Then my Lordy, we start to giggle. Woe! If we hadn't been raw civilians, in the brig we'd go.

Yesterday I achieved the doubtful privilege of becoming a section marcher. This was done by copying the Lieutenant's Army style of drilling. Hup, Hup, Hup, Har, instead of using Hut 2, 3, 4 the way most of the girls do. Now everyone is asking me where I learned to call hogs or coming up behind me and yelling Hup! Hup! Hee! Haw!

Oh, for my quiet & peaceful home life. As far as my flying goes, it's too early to say much. I've had $5^1/2$ hours on a PT-19A, which is a honey of a ship. We should solo them this week.

Didn't know exactly what to expect of the girls but got a pleasant surprise. A rather wonderful bunch on the whole. They've come from the farm, restaurants, Vassar, circus, universities, everywhere. A weird assortment of people. All the girls in my bay are from Miami. I was really lucky to get with them. We have much the nicest bay in W-7 (our class).

My time has come to go up. That…100 ton parachute is staring me in the face. My back!!!

Love, Win

HWS Dress Review

Fifinella

DAS WASP Fifinella

FIFINELLA WAS A friendly, lucky (though mischievous) gremlin originally designed by Walt Disney, and based on a character from Roald Dahl's book *Gremlins*. The WASP asked for permission to use her as their official mascot and the Disney Company generously agreed in January, 1943. So Fifinella went to war and was conspicuously displayed in various ways. She was worn on WASP flight jackets as a leather or cloth patch, painted on airplanes and on hangars, and even graced the main gate at Avenger Field.

Fifinella was a female gremlin and gremlins were known to do minor "naughty" things to aircraft, according to lore. It is said that victims believed these mischievous elf-like creatures were responsible for all kinds of mechanical failures and other problems. And they would play their pranks anywhere, anytime, on anyone.

The WASP had a song sung to the tune of "Pistol Packing Mama":

All the girls of Avenger Field,
Have got the bug to fly.
They take it off, turn it 'round,
And climb into the sky.
Oh, keep her straight and level,
Watch your altitude,
Happy, Fifinella,
Get into the mood!

PART TWO

WASP at
Camp Davis

The WASP at Camp Davis faced

difficulties and dangers with

little help from Cochran and

Washington, or the commanding

officer, Stephenson. They took upon

themselves the task of protecting

themselves as best they could, yet

fulfill their commitment as WASP. I

felt honored to fly with them.

– Ann Baumgartner Carl –

An Introduction
To Camp Davis

THE REGION AROUND Camp Davis and nearby Wilmington was home to several companies producing warships. As a result, the area was overrun with an influx of people seeking jobs. The North Carolina Shipbuilding Company employed 21,000 people in 1943 and produced two Liberty Ships each week. The railroads were essential for transporting soldiers and supplies. Wilmington and Camp Davis were both strategic war targets, and Nazi U-Boats were commonly lurking off shore where they blockaded ocean traffic from the Cape Fear River.

DAS Camp Davis Aerial Oblique

MMM Camp Davis Aerial

One of the most important training centers of the Antiaircraft Command and home of the Army's Antiaircraft Artillery School, Camp Davis was built early in 1941 at Holly Ridge, North Carolina. The camp proper was located on a 5,589 acre rectangular tract of land fronting U.S. Highway 17 and swamp land. It was renowned for its mosquitoes and other swamp pests. The camp and its related installations covered 44,434 acres. This area included a

DAS Camp Davis Main Gate

DAS Camp Davis Farnsworth Hall

JHU Camp Davis Theater

JHU Camp Davis Airfield – 1945

DAS Camp Davis NC Airstrip – 1990

Prisoner of War Camp and an airfield. Going into 1942, over 1000 buildings were completed and more continued to be erected as the need arose, as, for example, in 1943 when WASP arrived. At its height, Camp Davis had about 80,000 personnel.

In many respects Camp Davis resembled a city with its own government, courts, police force, utilities, churches, hospital, theatres, recreation centers, and stores. For transportation of personnel and goods there was a railroad station and an airstrip essential for Air Force use. The two Service Clubs were focal points for social activities. Each included a spacious lounge, a dance floor, a cafeteria and a library. And for moviegoers, the camp had five theatres.

At the Camp Davis site there are still in evidence two gigantic airstrips back in the trees. These runways span at least 100 yards in width and eight-tenths of a mile in length. The airstrips were used for training pilots, and for ferrying supplies and personnel in and out of Camp Davis. This was the airport for airplanes that towed targets for antiaircraft gunnery on Topsail Island.

WASP Selected for Experiment

The women being trained at Avenger Field had no idea that they would be doing anything other than ferrying airplanes. But Jackie Cochran realized that they had the potential to do many other flying tasks. General Hap Arnold decided that an experiment using women pilots at Camp Davis should get underway. The experiment would have WASP flying the planes that towed aerial targets, conducting strafing and other training missions, all of which required development of their skills beyond what training they had had at Avenger Field. 25 of the best pilots from the ferrying command were picked. The following excerpt from an official letter states:

> Confirming their verbal agreement Giles asks that 25 women be released from ATC/FD (Ferrying Command) for 3 months

'detached service' until transfers can be affected. The Air Staff request is authorized by Command of General Arnold: with the requirement that the women pilots be at least 5'4" and as heavy as possible.

Washington – The Pentagon, July, 1943

In July, 1943 a group of specially selected WASP attended a Pentagon level meeting at the posh Mayflower Hotel regarding some new assignments. Director Jackie Cochran looked serious, so much so that the excited chatter died away quickly. She described their next assignment, that of towing targets; piloting a plane with a crewman who would let out a long sleeve target on a cable for anti-aircraft gunners to practice shooting at. Most seemed excited about the challenge. To the question: *Do we have to do everything they tell us?* Cochran answered: *Yes, in the AAF you obey orders. Nothing can be more important to the future of the woman-pilot program than what you will be doing. It all depends on your success. Do your best.*

No sooner had this initial group been started on their way than Jackie engaged in preparations for a second group:

> Authorization is requested for withholding 25 WFTD graduates from the class graduating on August 7. These pilots are to be used on a special assignment which will be determined within the next two weeks.

Camp Davis Arrival

When the first group of 25 WASP arrived, they found that they would be working under the command of Colonel Lovick Stephenson who commanded the 3rd Tow Target Squadron. Stephenson had no use for women in the military, but he knew he had to follow orders. He no doubt saw them as a problem he didn't want to have. Their acceptance was less than enthusiastic, by some…in fact, downright hostile. The male pilots saw the women as a threat and, after all, if replaced it would mean the men would have to go into combat.

TWU Col. Lovick Stephenson On Right

Stephenson assigned the women pilots to administrative and tracking flights in tiny L-5 Stinson liaison planes and Cubs. They flew low and slow on tracking missions. Flying such missions in light planes was humiliating for these young women who had been trained to fly

TWU Jackie Cochran, Brig. Gen. Ralph Stearley Inspect

much heavier and more powerful planes. When word got back to Cochran, she flew her militarized Beechcraft to Camp Davis. She demanded that the women pilots get out of light planes and be given missions flying A-24s and A-25s towing targets. Lt. Colonel

Stephenson complied and after a number of other corrections by Cochran, the WASP were completely engaged.

As you would expect, the girls wanted to make their quarters habitable and attractive. One of their early tasks was to truck into Wilmington and shop for curtains and other amenities. Once they were into their flight work, however, their walls were decorated with maps and airplane identification charts.

A month later, the second group of twenty five, Class 43.4, received their wings and reported to Camp Davis. Two additional WASP arrived as replacements for the two that were killed in plane crashes. This brought the total WASP count to 52 at Camp Davis. Other air bases typically had 8 to 12 WASP. There is more about this in a later chapter.

Antiaircraft Artillery and Searchlight Training

CAMP DAVIS ACTIVITIES around the Antiaircraft Artillery Battalions cannot be discussed without the AAA Searchlight Battalions. The two are a symbiotic relationship, and they trained together to fulfil their respective missions.

There were two artillery firing points - Sears Landing and Fort Fisher. The main firing site was at Sears Landing, 4 miles from Camp Davis. The other major site was at Fort Fisher, 45 miles south on a historic Civil War battle site. A third site at Maple Hill in the northeast corner of Pender County was also named, but I don't believe they stayed there for any extended period.

A principal part of the camp was the AAA School. Classes were held for both officers and enlisted men. The curriculum included refresher courses in tactics and technique, and instruction in the technical phases of antiaircraft artillery.

Antiaircraft Artillery

The Antiaircraft Artillery is the branch of the U.S. Army dedicated to protecting ground forces and other static elements such as airfields and harbors from concentrated aerial attack.

WWII searchlights formed part of a system of aircraft detection linking locator devices, searchlights, and antiaircraft guns. The locators sent electronic information to the lights and guns which in turn tracked the targets in sync with each other. Once a locator locked on to an aerial target, the concept was for both lights and guns to be trained on the target. The target could be simultaneously located and destroyed. Locators were first based on sound and heat, and then later radar became the preferred method. Late in the war radar technology was integrated in both searchlight and antiaircraft gun equipment.

AAA training was done all over the country, but Camp Davis is where it originated.

Before WASP arrived, two U.S. Army Airforce towing squadrons based at the camp's airfield provided aircraft that flew thousands of miles each week, both day and night in missions along the coast. At night, the planes gave the 225th and other Searchlight Battalions practice in picking up enemy raiders in the dark, a job that they would have to do for real in England, and later on the continent.

Antiaircraft gun accuracy was at stake both tactically and economically. There was a lot of pressure to improve the accuracy of the lights and antiaircraft guns in order to be effective and use less ammunition...especially at night. Later in the war the radar would pick up the target, relay instructions to a primitive computer attached to the light, which would then track the target, finding it and illuminating it.

AAA Searchlight Units

AAA Searchlight Units were organized around the 60-inch searchlight: its power plant, the distant electric control station that aids in tracking targets visually, and radar that locates and tracks unseen targets. Searchlights had a dual mission, that of illuminating hostile aircraft for interception by U. S. aircraft, and for targeting antiaircraft guns.

DAS Antiaircraft Searchlight

GD Davis Searchlight Sound Detection

GD Searchlights Targeting

Lights were grouped into one of two classifications: they were either pick-up or carry lights. The pick-up lights, guided by data furnished by the radar, provided initial illumination. The carry lights locked onto the target to illuminate and carry it until the next carry light picked it up. The target was passed in this manner from unit to unit over the defended area.

Training at Camp Davis

All troops received instruction on how to fire a rifle and were required to practice this skill at a 1000 acre small arms range located 1 mile south of Camp Davis. Troops at Camp Davis also received more specialized training in coastal artillery. For example, instruction was provided in aircraft identification, the use of searchlights, and the firing of various sized guns – 50 caliber, 40mm and 90mm guns.

While enlisted men received specialized classroom instruction, much more of their training in anti-aircraft warfare was in the field. Training activities were often scheduled for the night hours. Searchlight units learned how to select positions, set up their searchlights, and camouflage their positions. At the same time, they were required to keep their rifles ready to fend off simulated paratroop attacks.

DAS 90mm Camp Davis – 1943

Antiaircraft training evolved and improved and, in 1943, new training methods were introduced at Camp Davis. The Women Airforce Service Pilots began training for target towing. On October 20 and 21 the female pilots and the 90mm gunners impressed the press corps with

TWU Gunnery Demonstration

their skills at a demonstration held at Camp Davis Airfield and Sears Landing.

Robert Clifton, an early tow-target pilot recalled that he and four other male pilots reported to Camp Davis replacing some old timers who had been out of school up to two years. They went through the gamut starting with the L-4 type planes dubbed "Junior Birdmen." He was initially trained in class 43B at Moody Field, Georgia, along with 203 other pilots. They graduated on February 25, 1943 and reported to Camp Davis two days later. During his stay at Camp Davis 2/26/43 – 5/44 they had 17 different types of aircraft – from L-4 to B-34s. All the planes were obsolete, some dating from the mid thirties.

Camp Davis was remote, hot, humid, and full of mosquitoes. It was not the most sought out assignment. For Clifton, it was pure luck. He was 65 miles from his birthplace (Faison, North Carolina) and could regularly take a plane home over the weekend. Colonel Stevens brought some men from Mitchell AFB to do some duck hunting at North Topsail. One of Clifton's more unusual assignments was to fly an L-4 Cub between Rte. 17 and the waterway. If there were no ducks near the duck blinds they had set up, he was to go where the ducks were and scare them over the blinds.

Wilmington was crowded and jammed with AAA and Marine Corps people so a plane was sent to Atlanta, Charlotte, Greensboro, Cleveland and other locations with some passengers for the weekend. Thirteen weekends in a row he ferried soldiers to Greensboro, 175 miles from Camp Davis.

Antiaircraft Artillery Ranges

The target towing mission was for AAA 90mm, 40mm guns and 50 caliber automatic weapons. Generally the AAA missions flew at 5,000 or 10,000 feet with 2,000 feet of cable from the airplane to the target.

TWU WASP A-24 Dive-Bomber Towing Target

Target requirements for the ranges were forwarded to the Operations Office. The mission board listed the range, time of start, time ending, pilot's name, airplane type and number. The tower reported the exact time the plane left the ground and that information was posted on the board about 10 feet from the Colonel's desk. Strict instructions were that the plane had better be off the ground at least 15 minutes before the scheduled mission time. The pilot was to check out the plane 30 minutes prior to the mission schedule.

After a briefing at flight operations, a WASP pilot and an enlisted man, who would ride in the back seat and operate the target sleeve and cable, climbed into a Douglas Dauntless dive bomber. They took off and once they were over the beach, the WASP was to radio the artillery officer in charge on the ground, as the cable operator began to turn the winch handle and let out the cable to which the muslin sleeve target was attached. The sleeve could be unhooked by a lever at the gunner's seat. When they had flown a couple of gunnery patterns down the beach, the pilot was to swoop down over the beach and the cable operator would release the sleeve from the cable so that the gunners could see the number of hits.

Antiaircraft Artillery Locations

The antiaircraft guns were aimed mechanically. A sergeant would estimate the range and enter it into the director. The director would calculate the angle of the muzzle. The 40mm rounds included tracers and could be seen by men who could move the rounds to the target by turning azimuth and elevation cranes on the guns by hand.

The first range used for firing at aerial targets was located at Sears Landing, a small peninsula located between the Intracoastal Waterway and the Atlantic Ocean about four miles east of Camp Davis. A road was constructed through a marsh to link Sears Landing with Camp Davis. A unique feature of that access road was a 75 foot retractable steel barge used to cross the Intracoastal Waterway and adjacent swampy area. Most of the training exercises at Sears Landing were brief in duration and the troops usually returned back to Camp Davis. As a result, only 22 buildings were located at the beach.

JHU Draw Bridge to Firing Point

JHU WWII Warehouse Firing Point

DAS Antiaircraft Gun – Sears Landing

DAS Tents at Sears Landing

The second range used for aerial target practice was Fort Fisher. According to a June, 1941 newspaper account, the Army had plans to use Fort Fisher as its principal firing point, but later amended its decision and decided to use the site for supplementary practice because of its distance from Camp Davis. Within a short time, Army officials had apparently changed their minds once again, because Fort Fisher did become a significant firing point for Camp Davis. According to one unpublished account, the former confederate Fort was re-activated for the first time since the Civil War to protect Federal Point, the tip of the Cape Fear peninsula, and Smith's Island from submarine attack. As the amount of firing practice at Fort Fisher increased, preparations were made to improve the facilities there. The firing point was located on the east side of the highway facing north, between the highway and the Atlantic Ocean. The Fort's utilities and living quarters were located on the west side of the highway between the highway and the Cape Fear River, north of the stone monument commemorating the Fort and the men who served there.

Specifications for construction at Fort Fisher called for the erection of 48 frame buildings and 316 tent frames. The tents had wood

DAS Firing at the Beach – 1943

floors and siding and were to be heated with army stoves during the winter. There were other buildings that would house support functions. An airstrip was also constructed at Fort Fisher. National defense took priority over historic preservation unfortunately resulting in destruction of a portion of the original fort.

New Experiences

For many soldiers their arrival at Fort Fisher was their first exposure to the beach. When the 391st Antiaircraft Battalion was assigned to Fort Fisher, the cooks found a considerable number of the men, many of whom were from the mid-west, unwilling to eat fried oysters or oyster stew. Not only were many soldiers unfamiliar with the pleasures of seafood dining, but they didn't know how to handle themselves in the surf and sun. Many did not know how to swim. Others knew nothing about the strength of waves and tidal currents. As a result, swimming lessons and beach safety instruction were introduced.

Soldiers Remember Camp Davis

What follows are reminiscences of soldiers who served at Camp Davis as antiaircraft artillery and searchlight men in their assigned duties. Their points of view about their respective assignments help us know what the WASP faced in their new missions.

Joseph D. Shinners, 232nd Searchlight Battalion: I arrived at Camp Davis in late 1942 as a young corporal assigned to the Artillery School to study a new tool of warfare, radar. We were quartered in the common two-storied barracks of WWII, and trucked to Sears Landing early every morning for training. "Cattle cars" we called the transports that bounced out to the sand dunes on the Atlantic. Cold, often dreary days of classroom and hands-on schooling…classified manuals and notebooks, chow lines, more classes, then another bumpy trip back to Camp, usually after dark.

The chow was not so bad, but we welcomed time off on Sundays and the opportunity to hit the Post Service Club Restaurant and stand in line for at least an hour for two eggs over easy with toast, for 30 cents.

One of our missions, as school troops, was training Officer Candidates. We took them to the field where they were to act as crewmen while we observed.

Athanan Landry Antiaircraft Artillery Battalion 776: When interviewed, he said he was a truck driver that towed 40mm and four 50 caliber guns. He remembers that they shot down several drones. It was costly so they stopped using drones for awhile. He also remembers severing some cables of the towed targets. One of their real challenges was moving and winching the guns in and out of the sand. Once his 18 weeks of training was completed, he was off to Camp Edwards, Massachusetts, and then shipped overseas.

Jim DeGuiseppi, Antiaircraft Artillery Battalion 559: Jim was an artillery mechanic for D Battery in 1943. He took his basic training combined with training on the 40mm guns and quad mounted 50 caliber machine guns. His group moved to Fort Fisher for more training and firing practice that summer.

Jim recounts: Gun Crew #1 of D Battery was setup and awaiting the plane towing the target, being the

DAS Jim DeGuiseppi

first crew at the left. They saw the plane coming at a distance and sighted in on it waiting for the target sleeve to show. Arthur Armstrong who fired the 40 mm was all set and the plane did not start to let out the sleeve until it was already in the firing area. As soon as he saw the sleeve he fired and was a little too fast, hitting the tail of the plane. He really should not have taken that chance but we were eager to hit the target.

This seems a plausible story of how Ruth Underwood's plane was hit, but Charles Nichols, AAA 465, believes they did the deed. I show both stories…could have been two separate planes.

Charles Nichols, Antiaircraft Artillery Battalion 465: Charles was at Camp Davis from October, 1942 to May, 1944, when his outfit shipped overseas. He was part of the school troops that trained OCS officers in gunnery. They drove halftracks with twin-50s, later quad-50s. A director would pick up the targets and direct firing.

He remembers that they put four 50-caliber holes in the tail of one of the planes. Later they found out that the WASP flying the target cursed them thoroughly. I believe it was WASP Ruth Underwood who chewed them out.

Charles said: We fired at Fort Fisher as well as at Sears Landing. In our firing we really got good at hitting the targets. But occasionally we would hit a cable. The drones were great fun. Our job was to lead the drone and fire close to it but not hit it. Too many times, the gunners would hit the drone and they would have to crash-land it. After a while, they stopped bringing out the drones. They were losing too many of them.

Once when General McNair was inspecting, the gunners impressed him by hitting the target sleeve then cutting it in half on the way down.

It was good duty at Camp Davis, but everyone wanted to go overseas to the war. In fact, when they got to Europe they soon shot down four German planes, no doubt an outcome of good training at Camp Davis.

Gustave Dubbs, 232nd Searchlight Battalion, January, 1943 to March, 1944: Gus was born in Bronx, New York on May, 1923. He joined the U.S. Army in January, 1943 and was stationed at Camp Davis, North Carolina.

GD Gus Dubbs – 1943

His unit was called the 232nd AAA Searchlight Battalion. The battalion was divided into four batteries: A, B, C, and headquarters. These batteries comprised about 160 enlisted men and officers. As searchlight batteries they were responsible for locating the enemy airplanes and illuminating them so the antiaircraft batteries could fire at them.

Battery A, for example, had three 268 radars, each of which was cabled to a control station that, in turn, was cabled to a searchlight operator. There were four searchlights for each radar unit. When a pip appeared on the radar screen, it was tracked until it was in range, and then was challenged by the radar crew. If the target was not able to properly identify itself, the command was to illuminate them.

Gus said: I was trained to track enemy aircraft using radar equipment. When the enemy aircraft was in range we illuminated them with our searchlights for the AAA artillery battalions. There was some form of communication between our Searchlight Batteries and the Artillery Batteries.

Our unit was sent to either Sears Landing or Fort Fisher for training. At these locations, the targets were towed by the WASP. The targets were towed on a long steel cable. We were supposed to light the target and not the plane. At one point we were sent out into field positions and bivouacked in various locations around Wilmington. While there was no artillery involved, we were supposed to spot the airplanes the WASP were flying.

GD Gustave Dubbs – Later

Target planes flew at various elevations and various distances from the shore. Our radar crew tracked them and when within proper range, the searchlight crew would illuminate them and follow a cable to the towed target sleeve using remote control mount with hand operated elevation and azimuth controls.

In 1944 our unit was re-designated the 762nd AAA Searchlight Battery and was sent to the Pacific Ocean area. After leaving the Army in February 1946, I took advantage of the GI Bill of Rights and went to college and became a Chiropractor.

During the past 30 years I have had the pleasure of developing and maintaining continuous contact with the troops that are still on our mailing list. I sent out 3 yearly mailings and organized Annual Reunions in various sections of Eastern US.

As the years have passed our reunions have had fewer and fewer attendees and they ended in 2002. Our Newsletters are now down to twice a year and the troop membership is about 25. I hope to keep the letters going as long there are troops to receive them.

John McKeown, 117th AAA Gun Battalion Battery D, March 1943 to October 1944: John was born in Lima, NY in 1924. He was drafted and entered service at Camp Davis, March, 1943. He was assigned to 117th AAA Gun Battalion Battery E and served there until transferred to Infantry in December, 1944 at Fort Bragg, North Carolina.

JAM John McKeown AAA

JAM John McKeown – Later

He believes all the AAA Batteries were activated at Camp Davis in late 1942 and 1943. The 117th was brand new with cadre from the National Guard in Wilmington, North Carolina. He says they were just scared kids at that time and he learned later that a number of the cadre were Lumbee Indians, with a First Sergeant named Novak, a Lumbee from the Fayetteville, North Carolina area.

One early method that John had for spotting planes was to use a long tube to follow the planes to help determine the height of the plane and target. This "height finder" information was then sent to the director who would guide the firing. Directions would be relayed to the 90mm guns. The greater emphasis for him was on tracking…not firing on the target. John said: *Our instructions were not to fraternize with the WASP, although many were tempted.*

In October, 1944 his outfit was moved to Farmingdale, Long Island to set up their artillery to protect the U.S. Coast. At that time the Germans were using their buzz bombs on England and there was much concern about attacking the U.S. After several months their unit was dismantled and converted to infantry troops for deployment to Europe.

McKeown was shipped overseas in February, 1945. Upon his return in 1946 he re-enlisted in the Army Reserves. Later called to active duty, he served in a number of assignments until retiring in 1980.

An Excerpt from Organization Day, 1944 Booklet, AAA 117th Battalion: The 117th AAA Battalion was formed in March, 1943. They were organized similarly to other artillery battalions, described above. They may have been located in this desolate swamp land, but the GIs didn't lack for entertainment by such people as Paramount's singing star Dick Powell and later by Joe Louis, the world famous boxing champion, who went a few rounds with GIs for fun.

The 18 weeks of training started with basics of M1 rifle instruction and target practice, and all the other basic training for survival skills. The fifth week of training took the whole battalion on its first bivouac at Topsail Inlet. It was the first taste of overnight camping for many of the men, but they went at it with determination. It was a good experience for these guys and made them feel like real veterans.

The ninth week saw the battalion move out to Topsail for their initial practice firing with the 90mm guns. The men were very effective for the first time out, and were all enthusiastic over the results.

The second practice firing was held at Topsail during the 11th week of training. 18 hits were scored out of about 400 rounds which was proclaimed a very successful shoot.

The 14th week of training saw the machine gunners get their

second chance at firing. The first practice, plus the additional work by all the gunners, resulted in a tremendous improvement, and many hits were made on the sleeve target during the firing.

As they approached the end of 18 weeks training, most were looking forward to being shipped overseas to the war. But they were also offered the possibility of staying at Camp Davis as trainers for AA. Some saw this as a lucky break and took advantage of it.

About this time the battalion had its first opportunity to hold a dance and a very successful one was held at the Service Club. Music was provided by the Air Corps Band, but during the intermission the 117th's own boys furnished the sweet and hot musical numbers. Their performance promised a lot for the future. Officers and enlisted attended the dance and the wives of both who lived in the vicinity were there. Additional girls from Wilmington, and many girls employed by the camp as well as WACS stationed at Camp Davis had a good time.

During the summer, weekend convoys to the beaches and to Sears Landing and Topsail Inlet proved very popular, and practically the entire battalion took advantage of the opportunity for the pleasant relief from its school duties.

In October, 1943 Batteries B and C gave a demonstration firing for the benefit of news reporters and photographers. The demonstration proved to be very effective; two targets were shot down, one with 9 rounds.

The battalion received a commendation from Major General J.A. Green who observed training at the AAA School with his staff officers in November. He reported: "The 90mm night firing by the school troops of the 117th Battalion was superior. The accuracy of this fire is convincing proof of their capabilities."

In November the outfit moved to Farmingdale, Long Island to set up their artillery to protect the U.S. Coast.

Justin Raphael, Officer Candidate School, OCS: Camp Davis had as a part of its training program an Officer Candidate School. These programs were a vital piece of military life as the growing number of recruits needed strong, capable officers to provide instruction and leadership. Justin Raphael was one of those trained at Camp Davis and his story typifies what these soldiers experienced.

Raphael was born in April, 1923 and grew up in New York City. In January, 1943 he was inducted into the Army at Fort Dix, New Jersey, then shipped to Fort Eustis, Virginia for basic training. After 8 weeks of training that included setting up and tearing down 90mm AA gun emplacements, he was chosen to enter an OCS prep school in a tent camp on the outskirts of Fort Eustis. Having passed the course, he was made a corporal and transferred to Camp Davis, North Carolina to attend the Officer Candidate School – OCS in May, 1943.

JR Justin Raphael – 1943

OCS at Camp Davis was a difficult and stressful testing and training period that was meant to make certain that officers who were graduated were qualified to lead. Many candidates were young and naïve. They were mostly in their early 20s. Justin was 20 when he was graduated as a Second Lieutenant on November 11, 1943. About 50% of the OCS candidates washed out.

Justin recalls: The last week of OCS was spent at Sears Landing for live firing of 40mm AA guns at drones. Only the candidates who would be graduated at the end of that week went to Topsail for the firing. Down the beach 90mm guns were firing. Suddenly we saw a plane enter their field of fire. We were horrified when it was hit. We felt terrible that the pilot and crew had to be dead. We were naive kids! The plane was a pilotless drone.

JR Justin Raphael – 2005

After graduation Justin was chosen to stay in Camp Davis and join the 576th AA self-propelled battalion in "Swamp Hollow," which was being organized to train as a unit. The barracks were tarpaper and wood on concrete foundations.

Due to its growing mastery of the air the United States no longer needed so many AAA officers. So in January, 1944 Raphael was transferred to the infantry at Fort Benning, Georgia for Special Officer's Infantry Training and further assignment.

In 1950 Justin married a local girl, Shirley Berger, and settled in Wilmington, not far from Camp Davis. He remains involved in veterans' activities in the American Legion and in the United States Volunteers, in which he participates in honor guard and veteran funerals.

WASP Assigned To Camp Davis

THE YOUNG WOMEN who came to Camp Davis as WASP are listed here in order that you can know who these vivacious adventurers were. A total of 1074 earned their wings to become WASP, and the best estimate is that about 450 of them are still living. The youngest of them are over 80 years of age.

52 WASP of high qualification were selected for the Camp Davis experiment that assigned them to high risk flying tasks. Of the 52 WASP, I was able to find 18 biographies. Those biographies are in the WHO WERE THESE WOMEN chapter. I have indicated those WASP that have biographies with an asterisk below. The middle name is their WASP name and the list is in order by WASP name.

Class	Name	WASP Name	Status
*43.5	Ann Baumgartner Carl	Baumgartner	
43.4	Mary Bowles Nelson	Bowles	
*43.3	Lois Brooks Hailey	Brooks	
43.1	Gertrude Brown Kindig	Brown	Deceased
43.4	Margaret Bruns Sliker	Bruns	Deceased
43.4	Patti Canada	Canada	Deceased
43.2	Lila Chapman Vanderpoel	Chapman	Deceased
43.4	Mary Clifford Lyman	Clifford	Deceased
*43.4	Alta Corbett Thomas	Corbett	

*43.3	Emma Coulter Ware	Coulter	
*43.3	Marcia Courtney Bellassai	Courtney	
*43.3	Betty Deuser Budde	Deuser	
*43.3	Dora Dougherty Strother McKeown	Dougherty	
43.3	Elsie Dyer Monaco	Dyer	Deceased
43.4	June Ellington Petto	Ellington	Deceased
43.3	Isabel Fenton Stinson	Fenton	Deceased
43.5	Elizabeth Greene	Greene	Deceased
43.3	Frances Grimes	Grimes	Deceased
*43.3	Marion Hanrahan	Hanrahan	Deceased
43.3	Elin Harte	Harte	Deceased
43.4	Mary Hines Grant	Hines	Deceased
*43.3	Lois Hollingsworth Ziler	Hollingsworth	Deceased
43.4	Catherine Houser	Houser	Deceased
43.3	Shirley Ingalls Thackara	Ingalls	
*43.4	Dorothea Johnson Moorman	Johnson	Deceased
43.5	Caryl Jones Stortz	Jones	
43.4	Kathleen Kelly Titland	Kelly	
43.3	Florence Knight	Knight	Deceased
*43.4	Martha Lawson Volkomener	Lawson	
43.3	Mary Leatherbee	Leatherbee	Deceased
43.4	Lydia Lindner Kenny	Lindner	Deceased
43.3	Bertha Link Trask	Link	Deceased
43.4	Constance Llewellyn Howerton	Llewellyn	Deceased
43.4	Nancye Lowe Crout	Lowe	
43.3	Frederica McAfee Richardson	McAfee	Deceased
43.3	Katherine Menges Brick	Menges	Deceased
43.4	Margery Moore Holben	Moore	Deceased
43.4	Eolyne Nichols	Nichols	Deceased

*43.3	Laurine Nielsen	Nielsen	Deceased
*43.3	Mabel Rawlinson	Rawlinson	Killed
43.4	Henrietta Richmond	Richmond	Deceased
43.4	Eileen Roach Kesti	Roach	Deceased
*43.4	Frances Rohrer Sargent	Rohrer	
43.3	Marie Shale	Shale	Deceased
*43.3	Joyce Sherwood Secciani	Sherwood	
43.4	Dorothea Shultz	Shultz	
*43.4	Betty Taylor Wood	Taylor	Killed
43.4	Viola Thompson Mason	Thompson	Deceased
43.3	Mildred Toner Chapin	Toner	Deceased
*43.4	Ruth Underwood Florey	Underwood	
43.4	Violet Wierzbicki	Wierzbicki	
*43.4	Helen Wyatt Snapp	Snapp	

* Designates a biography of this WASP is in Chapter "Who Were These Women?"

TWU Camp Davis WASP

Letters Home and A Journal

THIS COLLECTION OF Laurine "Rene" Nielsen's journals and Betty Deuser Budde's letters gives us a window into what their lives were like as WASP. The excerpts take us from their arrival in July, 1943 to December, 1943 and let us into some of their thoughts about their joys and fears, training, and being on assignment at Camp Davis.

Betty Deuser Budde told me to keep in mind that she was a young, homesick girl, and she wrote home often. Her letters reveal her intimate impressions and reactions to her time at Camp Davis. Laurine's journal entries were brief and usually technical. Both records are invaluable, giving us a sense of their day to day experience from both a personal and technical perspective.

Betty – Washington, July 21: Cochran had us all over to that huge Pentagon building today and General Arnold, yep, four star general, spoke to us in his conference room. It was a beautiful big room with red leather chairs and glass top tables and lots of windows, two big paintings and some trophy stands. It was a great thrill to have him there. The assistant secretary of war and a hall full of officers visited outside until we got through with our short session.

Golly, Washington's a wonderful place, not all buildings but lots of water, parks, the Potomac River, scads of historical buildings, big wide streets and the Capitol. Tonight Brooks and I and two others were down to the Lincoln Memorial and stood in awe in front of the big statue of Lincoln [remember Mr. Smith goes to Washington]. Also saw the Washington Monument and the OPA Building and all sorts of things.

We are awfully sleepy now and have to rest up for our trip down there to North Carolina tomorrow. We had expected to fly down in a B-34 but that was canceled so we'll probably have to go by train or bus and it's a long hard trip. No airline runs into that section of the swamps. We will be nearer the Atlantic and can go swimming as shores are near the base and there is a dance every Saturday night. But outside of that Cochran says it's pretty bad. We are no longer WFTD, but when we are named we may be called WASP. That's cute, huh?

...After the wonderful food and officers' club facilities at Dallas, this new camp is really awful, so we hear. Barracks, swamps, mud, dust, mosquitoes - but we have yet to make our own conclusions. The whole thing is an experiment to see just what jobs women can handle so the men can go to combat duty. So far, our physical and test at Bolling Field we have passed OK. Tomorrow we head for the swamps.

Betty – Camp Davis, July 22: We got off today after many delays and flew down in the C-47 [Army DC-3, Hap Arnold's own plane]. It was camouflaged and we had a whole ship for the 25 of us. The two young fellows who flew it had never been down to this camp before so we landed at Wilmington, North Carolina to ask where it was. We had passed it already. This camp is 30 miles north of Wilmington. It's near the ocean surrounded by swamplands and is the nearest thing to a war base that I've seen. If I didn't know better I would think we were somewhere in Africa near the front lines. The captain says the whole place was excited about our coming here. There is a whole gang of those out on the line to get a look at us. They've

HWS Camp Davis Snapp Bruns

been swell to us so far even to getting soap and a towel for each of us and putting up shades on our barracks windows.

The barracks rooms are about twice the size of our Sweet-water rooms. We're provided with mosquito nets too but no-body knows how to use them. The flying end of it sounds keen [we first have to be checked out in cubs]. But the living conditions aren't so hot. Of course we haven't seen the whole place yet but it's *so isolated*. 30 mi. from town – golly Ned! We have to get shots again Saturday so probably won't start fly-ing until Monday.

There are 2 showers and 4 johns for the 25 of us. The shower has no door. So your little dotter [sic] is fast losing all mod-esty. We have no wastebasket in our room [I'm rooming with

Brooks] but have army cots, table, closet with no door, and a thingamajig with 3 shelves, a sort of a bureau.

Rene - July 22: We're supposed to leave for Camp Davis N.C. at 12:00, but ship broke down. We finally left at 4:00 and arrived here at 7:00 pm. It's a huge place – 50,000 men – 500 in air force. They served us a buffet supper and we spent our first night in our barracks.

Betty – July 23: The flying sounds exciting with a lot of big ships and some interesting missions. They say we'll be kept plenty busy. On weekends after a while we can get cross-country trips either as pilot or passenger and stay overnight somewhere like Washington, New York, Florida, or maybe Boston. All depends.

Rene – July 24: Had a physical. Very simple. Then we all went to Wilmington by truck to buy curtains, etc. Had lunch in town. Truck picked us up at 4:00. We drove out past Wrightsville Beach and I had my first glimpse of the Atlantic from there. Started our decorating.

Betty – July 26: "Mosquito Hollow" is just across the airfield in among the trees. It's part of the antiaircraft school but a different section. They say the mosquitoes fly formation – two come in and pull the covers off and two more do the stinging. They are fast too. You can't swat them. There is a British unit here too. A group of Britishers who have been under combat fire. They are making a tour of the U. S. exchanging ideas on antiaircraft with our men.

Big antiaircraft guns are at Sears Landing and they practice every day. Machine guns and other types too. They are lined up along a beach. Then this plane flies by towing a sleeve target with about 3000 ft. of cable behind the ship. The guns aim at the plane, but by the time they shoot, the plane has passed – we hope – and they hit the sleeve target. That's one of our prospective missions. We haven't done anything yet except read tech orders and look over the ships. The A-34 is a big one which we hope to fly. They've promised us we could but the boys here say it takes a long time. And we had the same training they have, approximately. It's a heavy looking ship, a Navy dive bomber with 1650 hp. It's all camouflaged and has an awfully wide landing gear.

Rene – August 3: Link Trainer again. Under-secretary Mr. Patterson came today. Almost got up in A-24 but the radio was on the blink. Had cockpit check and test on A-24. Barracks inspection tonight. Some Colonel came from Washington to find out about our gripes.

HWS Link Trainer Camp Davis

Betty – August 3: I met some fellow from Oakland last week. He called last night and we made a date to go to dinner and dance in Wilmington tonight. He's going to borrow a friend's car. It's noon now and I was just informed that we're to have a meeting at 8 pm, so I can't go with the Lieutenant. Don't know how to get in touch with him either. He seemed like a nice guy. The fellows around here have been keeping the phone busy asking for dates, but this Lt. is the first one I'd consider going out with. This Sunday a group of us girls went to the beach. My suit consisted of a borrowed T-shirt and a borrowed pair of shorts. Looked silly but I got wet anyway. We rode out there in a staff car and back in two jeeps sent especially for us.

Rene – August 12: Flew formation, WOW, with Cerwin. Jean was in my ship. Really tight and kind of low at times. Most fun I've had yet. Had a sick engine which had me worried and landed in the rain. New meteorology teacher, Lt. Matson. He has impressive credentials. Tomorrow is Elsie's birthday. Hope her present gets here.

Betty - August 18: It's lunch time and I just got back from mess and guess what recording I'm listening to on Brook's phonograph – "Toccata and Fugue in D Minor," classical, huh? Funny thing about it is that I like it. She has several symphonic pieces and I'm getting so I can appreciate them. Still prefer Xavier Cugat though. I'd have you send some of my records if I thought we'd be here long enough, but there is more talk of moving some of us. Now listening to "Capriccio Italian" by Tchaikovsky, my favorite.

Betty – August 21: Yesterday on a cub mission, the air was so rough it shot me up from 900 ft. to 1200 ft. back down to 800. Gee, I was getting nervous.

Crazy Brooks had a cub mission too. Cubs are supposed to be soloed from the back seat. Well she climbed into the front seat without thinking then remembered it later, so while in the air she climbed back over the seat to get in back. Boy, I was nervous enough with the rough ride I was getting, to try anything like that.

Rene – August 24: Services for Mabel Rawlinson this morning. Very nice. [Rawlinson had crashed and burned at the edge of the runway on the 23rd of August, which left the women feeling apprehensive.] Met with Cochran at noon. She refuted everything we said. Didn't fly until late tonight. Just went up and flew around. My landings were off in the A-24. LINK for one hour. Instrument let-down. Hit Pittsburgh on the nose. Joyce Sherwood and Bike had a forced landing in #6204 tonight. They're okay. Ship burned on the runway.

Betty – August 27: Brooks' banjo just arrived so she's sitting on my bed plucking away. Ground school this afternoon sure was interesting. We went to the "ramp" in camp here, to investigate the guns and equipment which track us and simulate shooting. The system of height finding, azimuth, range and direction finders is sure interesting. The 90 mm gun can be run by remote control. Sure looks funny seeing the gun move around with nobody sitting on it.

Last night Marcia and I went to mess and Brooks didn't go cuz of her cold. She just wanted to rest. So she asked me to bring her a "snack." I got a whole dinner and as we had apple pie, I was going to bring her a piece. The guy insisted I take the whole pie! Said they'd just throw it out. So we had the whole thing and as a result had lots of company. Kids kept dropping in to listen to Brook's records and eat apple pie.

Betty – September 1: Saturday Marcia and I went to town. Brooks had won some records so we went to the music store. Well, we came out with eight albums and two separate records. Those two were mine besides two albums of Xavier Cugat congas. We really had a jam session that night. Brooks got a telegram today saying Cal Atwood was killed – he was my BT instructor, a swell guy. Brooks' roommate Anna had married Cal right after graduation. She was at Dallas, where I was first stationed. The girls at Dallas have had ferrying trips to California since I left. They flew some PQ-8s out. We have some here – little toy-like ships used in radio-controlled flight. One of the Dallas girls flew an A-24 in last evening, so we got all the latest news from her.

25 new girls came in yesterday – kids we had known at Sweetwater. I don't know how we'll manage with so many girls now. Our six week training period is supposedly finished, but we are supposed to have six weeks more experimental work "on the job."

Betty – September 2: You remember Joyce Sherwood, Mom? One of my roommates at Sweetwater, well her engine quit on her the other evening and she attempted to make a landing on the runway, but skidded and when she hit, the landing gear buckled. The ship caught on fire but she and her instructor jumped out. The fire didn't amount to much. She feels okay but X-rays show fractured skull in back. She doesn't even feel it!

Rene – September 5: Elsie and I arranged to go formation, but I lost her. So I flew. Had a dog fight with a P-47. Buzzed the trees until my seat dropped four inches. Flew along the beach at 0 ft. indicated. Missed first & third of my field landing for second time. Went swimming this afternoon. Frannie, Jean F., Jean P., Kay, Elsie and I. More fun. Had a beer at home and supper at the grill.

Betty – September 13: Last night the 4:30 siren blew. Brooks and I were in the barracks. Twenty minutes later, another siren blew. It just goes through you when the siren goes off because we know something's happened. A girl from the fourth class cracked up after landing. Killed. She had an antiaircraft Lieutenant with her. I think he is alive but had his face torn. The girl, Betty Wood, was married – a Sweetwater instructor last month – her head nearly cut off. I didn't see anything – not even the ship afterwards. It's funny how it doesn't seem to affect most of us anymore. People get hardened to it I guess. I still felt sick at my stomach, but I felt childish.

Betty – September 14: Today in peeling off to come down from my 10,000 ft. mission, I had the A-24 up to 191 knots which is about 220 mph, descending at 5000 ft per minute. Of course I didn't keep that up for more than a few seconds cuz that speed builds up too fast and it's a job to hold it back.

Rene – September 15: Solo local - met Daugherty over the Marine base and we did a little formation and rat racing. I had my crew chief along again. Very nice job.

Betty – September 17: This morning an A-24 came over the field very low with only one wheel down. They work on a hydraulic system so if that goes haywire, the gear won't come down. There is a hand pump too, but I guess that wouldn't work. So "Tony" Mildred Toner took it up high and just circled around trying to use up her gas so when she landed with no wheels it would have less chance of starting fire. Well, I hear the fuel pressure went out on her, so she brought it in for a belly landing. Made a honey of a landing in the dirt next to the runway and it just ground looped to the right. I haven't seen her yet, but they say she is OK and the ship just suffered a bent prop –

and scratched belly, of course. Well, I'm glad to know it won't always catch on fire.

Betty – Liberty Field, Georgia, October 5: This move was very sudden. I'm here with only a little of my stuff. This is a pretty nice place with trees and flowers, so different from Camp Davis. But we're surrounded by swamps and are about 42 miles from Savannah. Brooks, Bertha and I came down in the AT-11 yesterday about noon. I sat in the nose in front of the engines. It's a glass nose and has a swell view. Had to get out for take-off and landing though. Brownie and Lt. Clifton flew it so they could take it back last night. Most of the other kids arrived by car and plane today. Still a couple coming by train. There are 15 of us altogether. It's new deal learning about radio-control flying. I was just getting along fairly well with the heavy stuff, but now to come back to lighter planes... I'd rather fly the big ships. But it was a voluntary basis and I volunteered in a weak moment and talked Bertha and Brooks into it. I think it will be interesting though and after about six weeks we should be shipped off again. March Field uses the PQ-8s so that is my goal. How close I'll come to it is another thing. Probably get sent back to Davis! The rooms here are bare! Two cots in each room. No chairs or tables. In fact, nothing. Brooks and I got the best room with two windows. It's a corner room and looks out on a sweeping lawn – weeds.

Rene – Camp Davis, October 22: Cerwin checked me out in tow-target this am. When I got down, I was sent up again with a tow-reel man to have my picture taken releasing target. Halen was flying the O-47 camera ship. Never have been so close to another airplane. Three month anniversary today.

Betty – Liberty Field, October 26: Went to the show tonight and saw a swell pic – "Princess O'Rourke." I sure laughed a lot at

Robert Cummings! Nine of us went, which didn't leave many to go to the church services which were inaugurated tonight – to be held here every Monday night. Guess the chaplain thinks the Air Force needs looking after.

Today the radio control mission at 8,000 ft. had a sad ending. The PQ-8 got shot and the radio went out of control so the C-78 couldn't make it come down. It went scooting off towards Savannah all by itself and the C-78 chased it. There was nothing it could do to control it – the thing was set so it would fly straight or turn and it stayed up for 4 hours before the gas ran out and it crashed near Chatham Field just outside Savannah. In another case, a farmer saw one crash and a searching party was formed to hunt for the pilot who was never found, of course, because there wasn't any!

Pop, if you've been wondering where this career is going to end up, what do you think we're wondering? It seems as though we train for one thing and get it down OK, then train for something else. The new classes from Sweetwater are being sent to B-17 and B-26 schools! Are we jealous? The kids at Davis just got through getting a lot of publicity – in News Reels, etc, for their tow-target work.

Rene – Camp Davis, November 10: My first tow mission! It was fun. Fisher #1 at 1200 ft. Ran a tank dry and my motor quit just as I dropped the target. A-25 check-out. Shot 3 landings – 2 wheels, 1 – 3-point. It is not as wicked as they say. I like it very much. Remember that first takeoff when Form 1 hit me in the face?

Betty – Liberty Field, December 26: Our Christmas yesterday wasn't as bad as we had expected. We were all terribly homesick for weeks before and especially when it got too late to get home. But we had fun with silly little packages in the morning then had a turkey dinner at 1:00 pm and from then until bed-time the place was crowded with officers and their wives. We had open house so they could get to see our tree. They mixed eggnogs for everybody who all had a good time.

HWS Camp Davis Christmas – 1943

HWS AT-6 Tow Target Plane

DAS Thompson – Clifford – Lindner

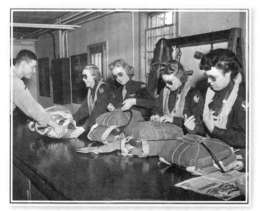

HWS WASP Checking Chutes

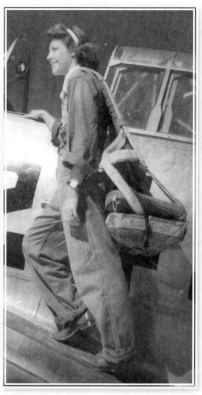

HWS A Climb to
Get In The Cockpit

DAS Mary Bowles Nelson

TWU WASP and Pursuit

HMS Last Minute Instruction

HWS Unidentified WASP

HWS WASP Fly Bombers Too

HWS A-25 – Helldiver

HWS Winter Flying Suits

TWU Dougherty – Sherwood – Knight

Recollections –
A Pioneering Spirit

FOR THE FIRST groups of women stationed at Camp Davis there was a clearly a sense of being pioneers breaking new ground. They had to learn to live in dormitory fashion, in barracks originally designed for men. They were assuming roles heretofore assigned only to men, training for and carrying out assignments women were not thought to be suited for. They were competing in a male arena and were acutely aware of having to prove themselves in every way. At the same time, the male personnel now had to adjust their thinking and their way of life on base.

This section consists of writings and conversations with WASP, illuminating, often with some amuse-

TWU WASP at Airfield Camp Davis

ment, those early days, and their encounters with their male counterparts. There was resistance and resentment on the part of the men, but much of that eventually turned to acceptance, camaraderie, and respect.

Lois Hollingsworth Ziler: They didn't quite know what to do with us when we got to Camp Davis. At first we were housed with nurses, and then moved to the WAC barracks. We first checked out in little two place Cubs and Stinson Liaison airplanes then larger ones. Eventually, we had our own barracks. I hung around the flight line to try to get checked out in various airplanes. It was there I first saw the radio controlled airplanes and got interested in them.

HWS Day Room Camp Davis

TWU Camp Davis Barracks

Helen Wyatt Snapp: I arrived at Camp Davis, a fresh recruit right after Mabel Rawlinson crashed and died. It was not talked about much as Cochran didn't want it publicized. There was another accident when the pilot came in wheels up [on its belly]. The pilot was OK but she was grounded and then taken to New York to face charges. Evidently, she was cleared and she flew the plane back to Camp Davis.

Marion Hanrahan: Colonel Lovick Stephenson, base commander, left no question as to what he thought about women in the military, especially as pilots. At first he was paternalistic advising us to go home and knit socks for the troops. After some accidents, both injury and fatal, he became more adamant that we should not be under his command.

Helen Wyatt Snapp: Camp Davis was a desolate base. There was no enjoyment except the Antiaircraft Officer's Club which wasn't very comfortable to visit. there was only card playing and drinking at dives around the base, where you wouldn't want to spend time. We often went to the beach when we could, and hung out around the barracks.

TWU Back Row (L-R): Mabel Rawlinson, Frederica McAfee, Laurine Nielsen, Mildred Toner, Mary Leatherbee, Jean Pearson. Front: Bertha Link, Katherine Menges, Florence Knight, Shirley Ingalls, Marie Shale.

For the unmarried, there was a lot of date potential and they kept a roster of names with comments like 'no' to this one. The reality is that most were ready to fall into bed by the lights out time of 10PM. And that was strictly held to and monitored by the "housemother." The "housemother" was responsible for the barracks, record keeping, and general order.

The quarters we had at Camp Davis were the best we had anywhere. Each WASP had a small private room [thin walls] and they shared a bathroom at each end of the barracks so there was little privacy. We even had a radiator in our single rooms. It was great for drying sox and underwear.

The WASP barracks were long and had a door at each end. If the doors were left unlocked, GIs seemed to think it was great fun to run through the barracks. They would run through with the girls scampering to cover up. They were probably doing it sometimes as a dare.

TWU (L-R): Lila Chapman, Dora Dougherty, Marcia Courtney, Betty Deuser, Emma Coulter, Elsie Dyer, Lois Brooks.

Lois Hollingsworth Ziler: When Mabel Rawlinson crashed, we were circling in the air and had to continue for an hour. We could see flames near the runway but they didn't tell us what had happened. When we landed, we found out that Mabel had crashed and died. There was talk about poor maintenance but we didn't want to refuse to fly, otherwise we weren't doing our mission.

Ann Baumgartner Carl: I knew that Cochran had selected her top pilots from Class 43.3 and later from Class 43.4 to prove that her pilots were professionals who could take on more dangerous jobs in the

MLV Camp Davis Matchbook – 1943

war effort. She promised the women that they would be flying bigger aircraft than they would be in the ferry command. This assignment was a crucial mission and their performance would affect the future for women pilots.

When towing a target sleeve, it was sobering to realize that the queer round blots of smoke outside the window were live ammunition exploding a bit ahead of the target. Some airplanes came back with holes in them.

Then at night we flew searchlight missions. That is, we flew a racetrack pattern at different altitudes while the artillery man tried to spot and follow us with their searchlights. This was essentially instrument flying. If you looked outside at the blinding light you lost your night vision and you couldn't even read the instruments.

Helen Wyatt Snapp: A vivid memory for me is of our barracks being right next to the runway. Before dawn the mechanics had the duty of warming up and testing the engines. So before our wake up call, this tremendous ear-shattering roar would have us all awake. We were presented with a hearty breakfast of greasy eggs and bacon, but I usually opted for a cup of coffee and a roll.

We were quite well disciplined and we marched everywhere. On the way to the flight line the mosquitoes would be just black on the pilot ahead of me and I knew they were the same on my back. But we kept marching. No mosquito repellent, but in the sun they didn't bother as much. The mosquitoes were most noticeable in the early morning and in the shade. Fortunately our barracks were screened and mosquitoes did not disturb sleeping.

We were responsible for six days of flying each week. If we

TWU Camp Davis Fightline – Oct. 1943

HWS WASP Marched Everywhere

were weathered out for a day or so, we had to fly the weekend to make up for it. We would wait at the flight line looking at the board for assignments. If no flight, we would go to the hard-to-control Link Trainer for practice, study and refresh our Morse code skills, or study to be up-to-date on the latest airplane information. Some of us were able to take officer training courses.

Lois Hollingsworth Ziler: We learned to tow targets over Sears Landing, at the beach. We would fly at lower altitude for the automatic weapons, and then in the twin engine airplanes, we would fly higher at about 10-14,000 feet for the big guns. It was pretty tricky flying with the ocean on one side and land on the other, frequently fog rolled in. We were shown the

HWS Camp Davis Towing Board

TWU WASP Clifford – Snapp – Thompson

TWU WASP A-24 Dive-Bomber Towing Target

safety measures at the firing line on the beach to give us some confidence that towing was safe. Also, every fourth or fifth bullet was a tracer that sparkled like a firecracker to show the gunner where his bullets were going. We would also go there swimming on weekends.

Frances Rohrer Sargent: Our as-signments varied. Mostly we flew target planes where an enlisted man would reel out a long sock of muslin on a cable as a target for antiaircraft gun-nery practice. I was checked out on ten different types of planes including A-24 Doug-las Dauntless, A-25 Helldiver, and AT11, B-34 and 37 and others. Sometimes we did div-ing exercises to simulate battle conditions of planes diving to-ward the guns.

FRS Fran Rohrer Sargent

A more challeng-ing flight at night was for training searchlight operators to spot and follow our aircraft at high altitudes. Search-light missions could be hazardous. The light is blinding and the pilot can become

FRS Frances Rohrer Sargent

disoriented. Having a good knowledge of instrument flying was a skill that I counted on. At other times it could be rather boring as you were to simply fly up and down for tracking exercises.

Marcia Courtney Bellassai: She recalled an Operations Officer who was quiet, but he really went to bat for them. Most offi-cers took a dim view of the WASP and even made fun of them

FRS Frances Rohrer Sargent A-25 Helldiver

at times. They put tough requirements on them and when they fulfilled them they wouldn't let them have the benefit of having qualified. The Operations Officer stepped in firmly and saw that they got credit.

Nylon rope was a new thing at that time. A long coil of nylon rope was dropped into Topsail Sound and just remained there for some time. Authorities wanted to see how the nylon rope reacted to seawater. WASP were given the mission to check on it from time to time as it was easy to see from the air in the clear water.

Marion Hanrahan: Marion was sent on a temporary basis from the Fifth Ferrying Group at Love Field to tow targets at Camp Davis for antiaircraft training.

When I arrived I found that the A-24s had been returned from the South Pacific because they were no longer fit for combat. Their tires were worn and weak, the instruments were malfunctioning and the planes were in very sorry shape. There were even some indications of sabotage that were thought to be the result of resentment of male pilots.

Pilots at Camp Davis flew certain antiaircraft missions at night to train searchlight operators and radar trackers, who would be trying to locate and shoot down aircraft on night bombing raids. Some WASP registered concern that the planes were not in good enough condition for night flying. In fact, some experienced male pilots were reluctant ever to fly at night in a one engine plane.

Mabel Rawlinson crashed. I knew her very well. We were both scheduled to check out on that flight in the A-24. My time preceded hers but she offered to go first because I hadn't had dinner yet. We were in the dining room when we heard the siren that indicated a crash. When we ran out on the field we saw the front of her plane engulfed in fire and could hear Mabel screaming. It was a nightmare.

Twenty-three-year-old Marion, who had been flying for nine years, befriended a couple of mechanics who then helped her understand some of their difficulty in doing their maintenance. She reasoned that they needed to work together for both of their benefit.

Later, some mechanical failures got her attention. There was an engine failure where she managed to limp back to the airport. Soon after, she started the engine of an A-24 and it ran so rough she taxied it back to the hangar. She consulted her mechanic friends and together, she having maintained planes since she was fourteen, they drained a cupful of water out of the carburetor. It seemed that this happened often, leading to speculation that water in the supply fuel tanks was a recurring problem.

Marion decided she had enough. She loved flying and airplanes for too long to sour a lifelong enthusiasm. Being a target at Camp Davis and forced to fly weary airplanes, Marion decided that this is not the way she wanted to serve her country. She wrote Jacqueline Cochran a letter of resignation. Cochran replied with a rejection of her resignation. She then went to her prior organization the Air Transport Command Ferrying Division who had released her for temporary duty at Camp Davis. Cochran blocked that request, knowing that Marion's experience was too valuable to lose from air assignments, but she relented, allowing her resignation under unclear circumstances. Soon after, Marion joined the WAVES.

Frances Rohrer Sargent: Fran recalled a frightening rescue while swimming at the beach in a riptide from which two fellows rescued her. *Wouldn't that have been something if I had drowned when my family was most concerned about the dangers of flying?*

Helen Wyatt Snapp: This was a secret mission and we were warned against talking about it. Perhaps it was, in part, because of the vulnerability of women as military pilots. But part of our job was aggressive flying in planes like the A-25 Hell Diver. Sometimes our mission was to dive for strafing the large gun emplacements. This was a daring maneuver, to dive to 500 feet so gunners could practice taking aim at a plane coming straight at them. Some women proved to be greater risk-takers than the men at strafing.

The whole program was threatened from time to time because of accidents and male non-acceptance of WASP as pilots, even though we proved to have a better safety record. The nay-sayers had to grudgingly admit that women pilots did an essential job.

HWS Helen Snapp Helldiver A-25

This was exciting work. Another mission was to take someone up to see if the gun emplacements had been properly camouflaged. Helen related something that haunts her to this day:

A fellow was really nervous about going up with me, but his superiors insisted that he go. I tried to reassure him and all went OK, and upon landing, I breathed a sigh of relief as he got off the plane. But even though I repeatedly cautioned him about where to walk safely, he walked right into the propeller. Fortunately I shut down immediately when I saw him go to the front and he only suffered a gash in his head from which he recovered.

Ruth Underwood Florey: The tail section of my A-24 was shot up on a towing mission. The enlisted man who was back there reeling the target for me shouted over the intercom that we had been hit and to get the hell out of there. It made me so mad that someone on the ground was goofing off that I sent them a few choice words about what they were using for brains. General Hap Arnold was on a surprise inspection tour that day and heard my transmission on the radio. He had to ground me for a few days but did tell me he couldn't blame me for my outburst.

TWU Ruth Underwood – Dorothea Johnson

Pilots were allowed to fly to other bases for dinner and dancing because the Air Force did not have an Officer's Club at Camp Davis. We were not too welcome at the Antiaircraft Officer's Club. It was an experience that only the young could do.

WASP towing targets for live ammo was one of the best kept secrets of WWII. We were not to tell our families what we were doing because it was a test of our abilities under fire. Finally we passed muster and information was released for publication to the public. Only women reporters were allowed on the base to interview us.

Our Commanding Officer Stephenson was notified they were coming so he had a store room cleaned out on the flight line. He had a table and chairs put in the room and hung a sign on the door - "WASP Nest." We were amazed as we had been ignored before this, by him. The men had a "ready room" where they waited for flight assignments, but it was "men only." We waited for our assignments in the dispatcher's office with chairs and benches. Then we were shocked to see the "WASP Nest" room disappear when the reporters left and we were returned to "peon" status. I avoided all contact with Colonel Stephenson because of his attitude toward us.

Ann Baumgartner Carl: The Camp Davis program was controversial from its beginning. This was Cochran's first attempt at placing WASP in other than ferrying jobs. Cochran's main concern was that these problems be kept secret. She demanded secrecy from the pilots and even extracted a promise of secrecy from mechanics. The basic problems here were prejudice against WASP and battle-weary airplanes difficult to maintain.

Yet despite all this, the women tried to make the best of it. They soon learned that to stay alive they would have to look out for themselves and they began to check their airplanes themselves. And they befriended the mechanics realizing they were suffering with combat reject aircraft and a lack of parts.

There was plenty of flying for everyone, as it turned out. There was even an interesting variety of missions to fly in several different types of aircraft, though never the big aircraft promised in Cochran's grandiose presentations. We started off flying a treetop level pattern over the camp to test artillery tracking. For this we flew a small L-5 Cub type airplane back and forth and round and round for several hours. Next we took four hour stretches at 10,000 ft., high as one should go without oxygen, in the A-24 Douglas Dauntless single engine dive bomber. We flew solo back and forth to test radar tracking for the gunner trainees. The seat got pretty hard after four hours and it was rumored that long exposure to radar made you sterile.

Source: *A WASP Among Eagles* by Ann B. Carl

Lois Brooks Hailey: Betty Deuser had an A-24 reserved to fly down to West Palm Beach, Florida and I had planned to go along. I tried to talk her out of it because I knew that A-24 was not fit to fly but she was eager to go, so we went. We got to West Palm Beach OK flying over the Okefenokee Swamp but we hardly had a drop of oil left. We filled it up with oil for our return trip to base the next day. The next man who flew that plane was a new Second Lieutenant Hinman. He went down in the trees with it as he approached the field and was killed in the crash.

Lois Hollingsworth Ziler: I just loved the radio-controlled mission. The way we learned was as teams of three. One person was in the radio control RC plane to make corrections. The learner with the beep box was copilot in the mother ship and the third was the pilot of the mother ship. Initially, I was the only girl interested in radio-control. The mission of radio-control was to fly unmanned as a target for the antiaircraft artillery gunners rather than having WASP tow targets. Gunners were to lead the RC plane as a target. Sometimes they shot them down or shrapnel would disable their ability to control the drone plane. Then they had a self-destruct button that would destroy the RC plane rather than have it crash.

Lois Brooks Hailey: We had an opportunity to train in a new concept. Lois Hollingsworth became interested in flying radio-controlled target drones, new at Camp Davis. She organized a group of 15 of us from 43.3 to move on to Liberty Field, Georgia for training in flying PQ-8A and later the PQ-14 radio-controlled aircraft.

The 15 women transferred from Camp Davis in October, 1943 for three months of training. They were: Lois Brooks, Patti Canada, Lila Chapman, Emma Coulter, Betty Deuser, Frances Grimes, Elin Harte, Lois Hollingsworth, Shirley Ingalls, Mary Leatherbee, Bertha Link, Frederica McAfee, Katherine Menges, Eolyne Nichols, Mildred Toner.

Helen Wyatt Snapp: We had a number of clothing challenges. To start with, we had no uniforms. For flight training we were given oversized coveralls that bagged but worked. Those who could sew would try to take them in somewhat. For dress, since we had the access to officer clubs and status, we were permitted to wear men's dress pinks and greens. That is, shirts and slacks. No jackets. Our uniform was a problem when we went downtown to Wilmington as women were not permitted in restaurants and stores wearing slacks. And nobody could believe that we were military personnel. There was even a case of where a WASP was arrested for impersonating an officer, because of the uniform and silver wings.

On top of that, women in the area disapproved of WASP for some reasons I cannot identify, presumably as military and in slacks.

Betty Deuser Budde: You know it has been a toss-up whether we are to go into the Air Force or the WACS. So when we heard that the bill was going before Congress, we decided we'd send a telegram to our representatives and let them know how we felt about it, thinking they would just be voting without much thought. Well, it kicked back. No sooner had Cochran heard of it, she called from Washington that very next morning, and bawled out the CO. So he bawled us out. He said we had no right to do it. Well, we thought as civilians we could wire our congressman if we wanted. And as long as Cochran is fighting for us to get into the Air Force, we thought we'd be helping her out. So we had to call all the four ferry bases and tell them to disregard the telegrams that asked them to send wires too.

We thought it was so funny! Couldn't help laughing about it, though the Major had made it seem so serious, saying it was "subversive action." He even went so far as to say some of us might be relieved of flying duty on account of it. Just let them try it! If that ever got to the newspapers, somebody could sure make a stink about free speech etc. Well, anyway, better not let this go any further.

Frances Rohrer Sargent: In March they gathered six of us WASP volunteers and Lt. Herbert O. Evans flew us in a bomber to Wichita, Kansas where the PQ-8 was built. The antiaircraft guys had shot down some remote controlled planes and they needed seven more. So we all flew out there and each brought a PQ-8 back to Camp Davis. The PQ-8 had no radio or navigation instruments so it could not fly in bad weather and had to stay under the clouds at low altitudes. They had few maneuvering controls as they didn't have movable flaps and

DAS PQ-8a

had a fixed tricycle landing gear. These were little short-range planes so their fuel capacity required them to make the trip in four-hour hops, frequent landings. One of them ran out of gas but landed OK on a dead stick and had to be towed from the runway. But they did it in a little formation of planes, completing the trip in five days. Those five days included one day they couldn't fly because of bad weather.

Dora Dougherty Strother McKeown: My WASP experience was a magnificent opportunity. I think that aside from the thrill of it, anytime that any of the women pilots flew anyplace, they felt they were representing women worldwide and for generations to come. We knew we were breaking barriers, and we had to fly our best.

"Women As Service Pilots" – An Interview with WASP

In February, 1944 an article titled "Service Pilots" by Alice Rogers Hager appeared in *Skyways Magazine*. The authors were on site at Camp Davis and they interviewed several WASP. This was an unusual opportunity for WASP to be publicized, as it was rare that reporters were allowed on site to talk with them. This is an excerpt from their article:

> Watch as a tow plane moves across the target course. The sky is misty and it's hard to see, but the complicated mechanisms of the gun crews have the range in a matter of seconds. The target, a simulated plane, is a safe distance from the tow ship. Isabel Fenton is flying today. As the monsters belched their leaden breath upward, the ninth round makes contact and the target blazing with the terrifying fury of a plane in its death throes spins drunkenly down until it plunges into the hissing of Atlantic waters. It is magnificent shooting, the kind of which brought down some 700 and more Nazi aircraft in North Africa and Sicily. It is more than that. It is a demonstration of American women at war for their country. Cold nerve, steady hands, keen mind and a willingness to do a job that takes patience and more patience. No glamour and no cheering crowds, just hard sober work and the kind of courage that can carry on when the probing searchlights blind you and you have to fly instruments to keep the course.
>
> That's the sort of women pilots Jacqueline Cochran has trained and is training to help the Army. I could tell you the aeronautical details of the work – how the girls made the transition from 450 hp ships to 1250 hp in a single jump, a move to "hot" ships that land at 110 mph. They are flying everything these days – these girls that the Army looked askance at, barely a year ago. Most of them had little more than 35 hours of flight time when they started their course at Sweetwater, Texas. They had everything to learn. They dug their toes in

and did learn. But they aren't through. They are constitutionally curious as all good pilots are, and they are hungry for more knowledge.

Yes…I want to talk about the girls themselves. They're worth it. They may not be overseas, but they are turning in extraordinary contributions. Several of them have even given their lives for their country when the planes they were flying crashed.

I'll give you a couple of them as samples. Helen Snapp of Washington, DC has a Lieutenant husband fighting with the infantry in Italy. Helen is dark, slender and very feminine. Her room in the barracks has frills and soft colors, but the walls are covered with maps and all sorts of plane identification charts.

"This is something that has never happened before," says Helen. "CPT was so limited. This means heavier ships and better equipment all the time. It was quite a jump to them from the basic trainers. The ships are heavier and not as sensitive, but they handle about the same."

Isabel Fenton of West Springfield, Massachusetts – who flew the B-34 – takes up the story. "I was scared stiff when they started me on the twin-engine stuff – we all were. Actually it's easier than single engines once you get the hang of it. Now I don't want to fly anything else. I've got over a hundred hours on them now."

"Are you ever afraid when you're flying for the gunners? Is there much vibration in the plane from the concussions?" I asked. "No," Isabel said, to both questions. "These boys are so good and the guns are so perfect we know we are safe. The fact that there is no concussion effect in the plane gives us additional confidence."

Isabel and Helen agreed that when the war is over despite their love of flying, when the men they have replaced come back home, they want to settle down and raise a family. Sure I want to keep flying Sundays and holidays. I think most of the girls feel the same way. It's going to be pretty hard to stand by on the ground and see someone else upstairs having all the fun.

Source: *Skyways Magazine* by Alice Rogers Hager

Radio-Controlled Drones

THE RADIO-CONTROLLED DRONE program at Camp Davis was experimental and classified as secret. Although rudimentary by today's standards, the groundwork laid by the WASP was an essential step in developing today's remote-controlled aircraft. The drones were isolated to their own secured area. The WASP involved were sworn not to divulge any information about the program to anyone, family, fellow WASP or friends.

When Lois Hollingsworth first saw the little radio-controlled drone planes, she wanted to know more about them. She knew

DAS PQ-8a

they were in a secret program at Camp Davis and that the program was not very accepted by the male pilots. Those in charge of the program welcomed her interest and very soon she committed herself to working with them. She became the first WASP to be involved with radio-controlled drone flying.

Radio-controlled drones were intended to be the next aerial target technology. Drone planes would be used in future for antiaircraft artillery practice, instead of the current method of towing a target on a cable behind a piloted plane. The drone would be more realistic as an aerial target and less risky than having pilots towing targets.

The drone program provided early knowledge essential to the development of today's Unmanned Aerial Vehicles - UAV. They are much more sophisticated now, and their capability allows them to engage in missions, such as high altitude surveillance and military attack controlled from miles away. The use of laser technology and GPS positioning precisely guides them. WASP were engaged in the drone program until December, 1944.

An Inside Look into the Radio-Controlled PQ-8 Drone:

In the bright red speedy little drones the women pilots sat on their parachutes. The planes were so small there was no room for a cockpit seat. The pilots' legs were extended with toes on pedals. Beside them, taking up half of the cockpit space, was highly specialized radio equipment. The little plane was controlled from a mother ship sending signals. Early drones were PQ-8s, called Culver Kaydets. They had only a short flight range, and had to be landed and refueled often.

For a perspective on size:
Drone - PQ-8 is 17 ft. 8 in. length; 26 ft. 11 in. wingspan; 1300 lb.; 116 mph speed
Mother - UC-78 is 32 ft. 9 in. length; 41 ft. 11 in. wingspan; 5800 lb.; 175 mph speed

Trainees in the mother ship, L-1s early in the program, would learn to fly the drone remotely, while a WASP would ride in the drone as safety pilot. If the person being trained made a mistake, the WASP in the drone could recover it. The mission was dangerous and only a few WASP agreed to fly the drones. Trainees practiced maneuvers and landings with a WASP as backup pilot in the drone - a nerve wracking job to say the least. Of course, during actual use as a target, no one was in the drone.

Helen Snapp said that crashes were frequent while they were learning the controls and she would often ride in the drone as backup pilot in order to recover it if the trainee screwed up and she could land it. *I just loved this little plane. It just hugged you and I felt a part of the plane. If there was any kind of plane I could pick to own, it would be one of these. They were our "babies."* Helen did suffer a broken nose in one of the landings, but it didn't change her mind about the assignment.

As the drone plane was developed it became increasingly powerful. The mother ship had to be upgraded to keep up with it and so UC-78s were used.

Some WASP Recall Their PQ Experiences

Lois Hollingsworth: Along with others from Class 43.3, I was sent to Camp Davis to tow targets. I became interested in the little red planes at one end of the airfield. They were Culver Kaydets with fixed tricycle landing gear that had been converted to radio-controlled planes. I soon found out that they were being flown out over the ocean for antiaircraft guns to fire at. Since I showed that interest, I was asked if I wanted to learn how to do it.

In August I checked out in the little plane, learned to fly it, then engaged in auto-pilot procedures connected to radio control, and learned to use the switches…they called them beepers…that would send signals for the plane to follow your commands.

Commands were full throttle, half throttle, turn left, and turn right, throttle back, nose up, nose down and brakes. Once I learned the controls and the servo controls, I would sit in the back seat of the L-1 'mother ship' and fly the PQ-8 while another pilot was flying the L-1 in close formation.

While learning to fly the PQ-8 there would be a safety pilot in the PQ-8 in order to recover it if the student at the beeper controls erred. After being checked out we continued practicing landings. Then I was ready to fly some actual missions. There would be no one in the little Culver…they called those flights nullo flights, meaning no one in the plane. I flew a total of 5 missions at Camp Davis, only one of them did I make a successful landing. Two of them were shot down in the ocean, and two of them I couldn't get landed right because of some kind of damage to the controls. The gunners were not supposed to shoot them down, just aim ahead of them, but sometimes flak damaged the planes.

Shortly after that, we got new target planes called PQ-8A that were faster and the L-1 couldn't keep up with them so we switched to the Cessna UC-78 as a chase plane. Then several of us pilots in the radio control group practiced with this new airplane. Eventually we were all checked out with this new plane and we practiced and took our turns as safety pilots for other trainees.

Later, four of us, two men and two women, were sent to Dry Lake where radio controlled flights were to carry bombs on board and they would be flown into a remote target. This plane was a larger radio controlled PQ-14 that had a larger engine that carried a bomb payload with a TV camera in its nose so the target plane could transmit what it was seeing to the mother ship. The person in the mother ship would direct the plane to the target on the mountain side that had a weird outline of a military target of some sort. The mother ship was about five miles distant and even though we could barely see it, the target was successfully hit. Later, changes were made to use radar rather than TV to guide the plane.

In October, 1943 fifteen WASP left Camp Davis and went to Liberty Field in Georgia for radio control work. They practiced every day on that assignment. One would pilot the UC-78 and, as co-pilot, another would control the drone with the beeper box. By the middle of December we all could control the plane without a safety pilot, and we made our first successful nullo [without pilot] landing. Two PQs were shot down and two attempted landings crashed, due to lost beeper control or flak in the control mechanisms. One success out of five was fairly typical. After Christmas we returned briefly to Camp Davis, and then the three groups of five each were sent to El Paso, Texas, Massachusetts, and California. I went to El Paso.

Betty Deuser: Lost another PQ on a mission. That's four in a row. One landed OK but didn't have any brake control and cracked up off the runway. The last one was shot and out of control – landed in a tree just north of the field. One new one came back, the radio control still perfect but the wings well ventilated. Found a couple of pieces of the shrapnel in the ship. We've been flying three-ship formation in the A-25s lately. It's fun but calls for much concentration.

Yesterday I missed dinner because I flew the PQ mission late. None of the girls have flown the C-78 on a mission here yet. Shirley was going to fly it while Lt. Potts beeped, but she had planned to go to Charleston at 4 pm so he asked me to fly for him. Was interesting. Cold at 9,000 ft. though. When it was almost time to come down, the generator fuses on the C-78 burned out and that takes the PQ control off so the PQ went flying along straight and I chased it for about 10 miles while we changed fuses. The fuses should've been 50s but we only had 40s so I had to keep turning the generator switches off so the fuses wouldn't blow again. Turned them on long enough to turn the PQ and then off again and on again for each beep. Got it back at sunset and Potts made a nice landing.

A drone story is told that during one of the test flights, a pilotless radio-controlled PQ-8 was hit by shrapnel but continued to fly out of control. It eventually crashed and a farmer saw it go down. He organized a search party to look for the pilot. Of course, they never found one.

Lois Brooks: Lois Brooks recalls that after finishing their training at Liberty Field, Georgia, in December, 1943 they were given orders to report to three different locations. Five went to Otis Field, Massachusetts, where Frannie Grimes would be killed in an A-24. It was carburetor ice and the engine choked on takeoff. Five went to March Field in California, and Lois Brooks, Emma Coulter, Betty Deuser, Lois Hollingsworth and Kay Menges were assigned to Biggs Field in El Paso, Texas. It was a good assignment primarily flying radio-control PQ-8 target planes, but they also did lots of night flying in the twin Beech for searchlight targeting. They also had other missions strafing the men in bivouac in the desert, buzz jobs, radar tracking, towing sleeve targets in the B-34, and taking antiaircraft officers up for observation flights. The PQ-14 came in to replace the PQ-8 radio-control and a C-47 Beechcraft was assigned to keep up with the faster drone.

Lois Brooks said: I had a mishap on a PQ-8 training flight. We had been at El Paso for a week before getting our first radio-controlled flight. Our flight leader sent us out on Sunday to the practice area – Condron Field north of El Paso. Kay Menges flew the mother ship, a C-78, Betty Deuser was the "beep pilot" and I was backup pilot in the PQ-8. I could take over if the radio-control beeper failed. We made a good landing and prepared to take off. The field was a large square dirt field. During the week men were there, but on this weekend none were to be seen. We lined up "Baby Bird" and "Mama Bird," Betty gives throttle and "Baby Bird" jammed left rudder and shot across in front of "Mama Bird!" I should have cut the whole operation, but instead I planned to take off manually. I saw a ridge of dirt across my path. I had 60 MPH and hoped I can lift off before hitting the ridge – about four inches high. No luck, I broke the nose wheel of the tri-cycle landing gear and flipped the PQ-8 on its back. Betty and Kay tried to roll the target plane right side up, but they could not. Betty stayed with me and Kay flew back to El Paso to get help. I was upside down hanging on a safety belt for 50 minutes. Men came back with Kay and they chopped me out. Luckily, it didn't burn. I had broken my two upper front teeth and it would be some time before the Air Force could decide if they should replace them. Finally I got a solid gold plate and two teeth.

Lois Hollingsworth: Our duty at El Paso was good and I appreciated being in my own bed every night. The girls who ferried planes flew all over the country never knew where they would be sleeping. We also had permission to take an available aircraft for the weekend if we stayed within 600 miles. They were usually nice twin Beeches and I remember flying to Tulsa twice as well as other fields.

My first mission was in January, 1944. In April we began using the PQ-14. This was the plane that was used in October's test to carry explosives. It had twice the horsepower as the PQ8, had retractable landing gear, and flaps. All those were different and had to be worked in a different way with the beeper controls. All those new operations had to be controlled with the beep box. After April we did a lot of practicing, because we were very close to El Paso we would fly about 30 miles north to what they called Conders' Field, later, White Sands, and practice our take off and landings there. At that time the field was very primitive.

The PQ-14, being very fast, required them to switch from the UC-78 to a twin Beech usually a C-45 or an AT-11. The ground crew would taxi the plane out to position, the mother ship would beep signals to the target ship to be sure all the controls were working. After checkout, it would take off, raising the landing gear. Then they would set it on course to its range, maybe 14,000 ft. for the big antiaircraft guns and sometimes to a lower altitude for automatic weapons. The mother ship would put it on a parallel course with the firing range then the mother ship would peel off. They would run the course, turn the plane and come back up the range for a couple of hours.

When you flew a target mission you would take the little radio-controlled plane out in front of the guns and then you would peel around behind the guns, speed up, catch the little airplane, turn around, send it back again, and they would shoot at your baby. If they didn't hit it, then you would collect it an hour later and land it. They were supposed to use the little plane as a moving target, but fire ahead of it. These radio-controlled planes were costly. But they did get shot down at times. And sometimes the drone plane would fail to respond. Control was limited to steering it out over the Texan desert where a self-destruct charge would destroy it. As long as they could control the PQ, they would bring it back to the base and land it.

Source: Texas Woman's University, Video of Lois Zilers' discussion about PQ-8 Radio-Control Drones.

Other Remote Controlled Pilotless WWII Attempts:

During WWII, in England, the bombing missions targeting the German VI rocket launch sites brought innovations in remote controlled flight. Combat worn B-17s that would be otherwise scrapped were taken and converted into drones that carried a payload of 9 tons of explosives. The auto pilot could be controlled remotely by another B-17. A TV camera would monitor the gauges and flight instruments. A second TV camera in the nose showed the controlling pilot what the drone "saw."

A pilot and co-pilot flew the drone plane to the English Channel, armed the explosives, and bailed out. The controlling plane flew at some 10,000 feet and monitored and maneuvered the drone plane flying at 2000 feet. They would fly it to the target and nosedive it into the German site. They had some successes, but the bombing missions carried out by piloted bombers were more devastating to the well barricaded installations. Joe Kennedy, John F. Kennedy's older brother, was killed on one of those missions.

*I*f I die violently, who can say it was before my time? I want no one to grieve for me. I was happiest in the sky – at dawn when the quietness of the air was like a caress, when the noon sun beat down, and at dusk when the sky was drenched with the fading light. Think of me there and remember me, I hope, as I shall you.

– Cornelia Fort, First Woman Pilot to die in military service, March 21, 1943 –

Crashes

IN ALL, THERE were 38 WASP fatalities, 2 of them occured at Camp Davis. All the Camp Davis accidents and fatalities are listed here, along with more description about Mabel Rawlinson, Betty Taylor Wood and Joyce Sherwood Secciani's crashes and accident reports.

While no one likes to dwell on them, plane crashes were an inevitable part of the war effort, and occasionally did occur in non-combat situations. As for those that happened to some of the WASP and their flying mates, there was speculation as to the reason. Pilot error is always called into question, but in the case of many planes being used in training programs, they were well-worn and prone to having mechanical problems. Praise should be given to the mechanics who did their best to keep aircraft flying safely. Early in the WASP program there were rumors of sabotage in one or two crashes, but that was never documented.

Mabel Rawlinson

Mabel Rawlinson, 26 years of age, was killed when she crashed at Camp Davis in the swamp at the edge of the runway on August 23, 1943.

Her assignment at Camp Davis was towing targets for antiaircraft gunner training. Additional training for the A-24s included night flying. On one of these night flights mechanical problems forced the plane down. It hit some pine trees surrounding the field and nosed down, hit the ground and split in two. The instructor in the back seat was thrown clear. Mabel was trapped in the front of the plane as it went up in flames. The canopy release for her cockpit was known to be difficult from the inside. The A-24s they were using for tow target training were worn out from war duty and were difficult to maintain.

No compensation was available to the Rawlinson family because WASP were considered volunteer civilian pilots, not military. Transportation of her body and funeral expenses were borne by the Rawlinson family with assistance from fellow WASP contributions. Ms. Rawlinson was honored with an American flag draped over her casket, and the Kalamazoo Civil Air Patrol honored her with buglers, fly-overs, and solemn gun salutes.

Rawlinson Accident Report Summary: The following excerpt is based on the text from the Army Air Force Accident Report No. 129, dated September 4, 1943. The report was provided by Craig Fuller of Aviation Archaeological Investigation & Research:

Mabel was on a night training flight with her instructor 2nd Lt. Harvey J. Robillard. This was her first night flight at this base and it was about 9 PM.

Prior to this flight, Mabel had accumulated just over 200 hours of flight time in the WASP. This was in addition to her flying time prior to joining the WASP. A little over 10 of these hours were in an A-24 like the one they were flying this night at Camp Davis, North Carolina.

According to 2nd Lt. Robillard, who was seriously injured during the crash, "We were circling 2,999 feet at South Zone at about 2100. The tower called and told us to shoot a landing on Runway 4. She entered the pattern normally at 1100 feet and let the wheels down. Soon it seemed something was wrong. I felt the throttle moving back and forth and realized the engine was dead. By that time we had 700 feet and were across runway and there I took over and told the student to jump. I then shouted at the student to jump. I had little time to look and see if she jumped. Somehow I knew she hadn't. I attempted to bring the plane in for a crash landing on the end of Runway 4. The next thing I felt the airplane shudder and I remember no more."

The AAF report summarized various reports with the following: Halfway through the first attempt to bring the plane in wheels down, he ordered the Woman Pilot to jump. He finished the first 90 degree turn, flew an abbreviated down wind and base leg, and was trying to round out a turn on to final approach when the plane crashed into the trees from a half stall in turn at low altitude. The plane broke into halves at the fuselage at the point of the rear cockpit. The safety pilot was thrown clear but the plane burned. The woman pilot did not jump and was burned to death strapped in the cockpit. The wrecked plane rests about 399 yards from the end of Runway 4. A wide drainage ditch and jungle like trees and swamp undergrowth handicapped rescue efforts.

There is no mention in this report of a faulty latch in the front cockpit where Mabel was seated. So it is left to unofficial documents to speculate.

Betty Taylor Wood

Betty Taylor Wood, 22 years of age, was killed in a landing accident on September 23, 1943.

During a landing at Camp Davis with the camp's chaplain on board as a passenger, she had to abort and give her A-24 full throttle to go around for another try. But the plane rolled and dived into the ground. Both Betty and the chaplain were crushed between the canopy and plane. It is said that the throttle was sticky and when she hit full throttle the delay allowed the wheels to hit the runway and the plane rebounded then torqued the aircraft over with the late surge of power. This pushed the A-24 into the ground.

Cochran investigated Betty Taylor's accident. After the funeral the next afternoon, she left Camp Davis without a word about her findings. What she had uncovered could not be discussed. And she had asked mechanics with whom she had made the discovery to keep quiet and not to alarm the girls. If they found out, Cochran feared there would be a negative reaction far worse than that after Mabel Rawlinson's death, and the entire WASP program might be in jeopardy. Cochran was convinced the accident was caused by sabotage, sugar in the gas tank.

Joyce Sherwood Secciani

Just two days after Mabel Rawlinson's death, classmate Joyce Sherwood also had engine failure in an A-24. According to the Army accident report, Joyce and the instructor managed a belly

TWU Joyce Sherwood Crash

TWU Joyce Sherwood Walked Away

landing, the engine detached from the rest of the plane, the plane caught fire after stopping, and both Joyce and her instructor suffered minor injuries, but no burns.

There was little else to be discovered in documents about Sherwood's accident, since no serious injury resulted. But it is an event that deserves noting among the crashes.

Comments by Fellow WASP

In a documentary film interview a former WASP, Dora Dougherty, said: Mabel Rawlinson's death at Camp Davis…I don't know exactly what it could be attributed to. I did not go out to the crash scene, but the fire was intense. They could not get Mabel out and she burned. It was a very traumatic time for all of us there. I remember there was an old nurse who came over to our barracks and she had a couple bottles of beer and she sat on the end of the barracks out there watching the fire. Drinking her beer and singing old hymns … in a deep sort of whisky tenor. Now I think when you join the military you obviously go through a mind set that you are prepared for something like this. This was the first time that I had seen a friend die. So it was a trauma for me and I think for all of us.

Marion Hanrahan wrote: The women pilots were, in fact, placed in harm's way by towing targets for training ground troops. Since these ground troops were "in training", it is certainly possible that they could miss their targets. It is also true that most of the female pilots encountered overt resentment from some of the male pilots that did not want to be shipped overseas.

A-24 Accidents

The real causes of accidents were difficult to determine. The A-24s they were using for tow target training at Camp Davis were worn out and not well maintained due to lack of parts, and they were being fueled with 90 octane vs. the 100 octane required. Eleven of the fourteen accidents at Camp Davis involved the A-24 and are detailed below:

Airplane Accidents At Camp Davis

Date	WASP	Class	Airplane
8-06-43	Elsie E. Dyer Monaco	43.3	A-24A
8-23-43*	Mabel V. Rawlinson	43.3	A-24A
8-25-43**	Joyce E. Sherwood Secciani	43.3	A-24A
9-13-43	Mildred A. Toner Chapin	43.3	A-24A
9-15-43	Lila Chapman Vanderpoel	43.2	A-24A
9-23-43*	Betty Taylor Wood	43.3	RA-24A
10-18-43	Lydia D. Lindner Kenny	43.4	RA-24A
10-25-43	Mary Bowles Nelson	43.4	RA-24B
10-25-43	Viola Thompson Mason	43.4	RA-24B
11-18-43	Nancye Lowe Crout	43.4	RA-24A
12-09-43	Henriette M. Richmond	43.4	AT-6A
12-21-43	Mary Hines Grant	43.4	AT-11
1-07-44	Henriette M. Richmond	43.4	RA-24A
2-04-44	Lydia Lindner Kenny	43.4	RA-25A

Notes:

* WASP Fatal Crashes

** Aircraft Broken in Two Pieces – WASP Not Seriously Injured

Sources:
Crash information provided by Andy Hailey, February 21, 2005
www.creasonwings/mabel.htm

PART THREE

WASP
Then and Now

It was a magnificent opportunity.

I think that aside from the thrill of

it, anytime that any of the women

pilots flew anyplace, they felt

they were representing women

worldwide and for generations to

come. We knew we were breaking

barriers, and we had to fly our best.

– Dora Dougherty Strother McKeown –

WASP Adventures

THESE ARE STORIES that must be included in any WASP history. They are beyond the Camp Davis experience, but they are adventures that reveal the outreaching spirit of these women.

A P-51 Ferrying Venture

One of the ferrying routes delivered planes to Newark, New Jersey. Carole Fillmore was given her first P-51 Mustang to deliver there.

As it was winter, she flew a southern route across the country intending to turn north up the East Coast to avoid inclement weather. Her first day, she flew all the way from Long Beach, California

DAS P-51 Mustang

to Athens, Georgia, where she ran out of daylight. But, when she tuned in the Athens tower and called for landing instructions, no one answered. She called the tower again and still received no response. In minutes she was directly over the field.

She began to circle and asked for a radio check. Suddenly an exasperated voice rasped into her earphones: *Will the woman who is calling please stay off the air, we're trying to bring in a P-51.* Carole looked around her in the growing dusk for the other Mustang. Seeing none, she called in again for landing clearance. *Will the lady who's trying to get in please stay off the air!* The tower controller shouted. *We are trying to make contact with a P-51.* Patience running out, Carole declared: *For your information, the lady who is on the air is in the P-51,* and she headed straight down the center of the runway at 120 mph. to a perfect landing. *Aw, that was beautiful,* drawled the tower. She taxied to the flight line, to scores of young cadets pouring out of the ready room to gawk at the huge new fighter they all dreamed of flying someday. *It's a girl,* someone shouted as she climbed out of the cockpit. She stood on the wing as they cheered and felt like Lindbergh had just landed.

Source: *The Wonderful Women in their Flying Machines* by Sally Van Wagenen Keil

Showing What They Could Do

The girls were delivering several Stearman planes to California when they landed at a small airport just jammed with pilots headed overseas. At lunch there was a lot of kidding about the little biplanes and the girls said: *OK, just you watch us take off.* What an unbelievable spectacle! Despite knowing it was against the rules, those three girls lined up and you could see they were holding on the brakes while pushing the throttles until the planes actually got their tails up and then roared forward almost side by side, keeping the planes close to the ground to the end of the runway, then zoomed up in a steep climb, one peeling off in a turn to the left and the other to the right and the middle one straight ahead. That was bad enough, but then they did a wingover and dived right back down, so low over the men that they scrambled or fell flat, the WASP waving wildly and you could see them howling with laughter. The girls thought they had proved something to the guys.

Ann Baumgartner Carl's Recollection

Ann was one of the WASP assigned to Camp Davis where, initially, the women were not well received.

She recalls: The varied flying and the building up of flying time experience were the pluses in the assignment. And there was one more perk. In any free moment from target flying, we were urged to take an aircraft on a cross-country flight to exercise our cross-country skills. Sometimes we would go off three or four at a time, practicing formation flying on the way. Once we flew to Kitty Hawk at Mateo Island, landing on the short simulated aircraft carrier runway. When we slid back our canopies, unbuckled, and climbed out of our Curtis A-25 dive bomber, the linesmen came out to check us in, but suddenly stopped. *Girls!* They shouted. *And what can we do for you ladies?*

What a pleasant surprise compared to Camp Davis! *We'd like some fuel please, and a look at your base here. Is this really where the Navy pilots practice carrier landings?* We asked. One replied: *Yes, indeed, so you can consider yourself carrier pilots now.*

Then we had to explain who we were. I don't know why they believed us in our two-sizes-too-big flying overalls. When we signed in at the office, the officer in charge was equally amazed: *Those are Navy SB2Cs aren't they?* I told him they were Air Force versions without the folding wings the Navy needed.

They shouted: *Come back again*, as we climbed back into our "carrier" planes.

On another outing, solo, returning to the field, I flew all the way at treetop level, following the contour of hills and valleys, over barns and animals in their fields. I was going about 180 mph, but it felt like 300. A foolish and illegal performance, but exciting!

Ann Baumgartner left Camp Davis in February, 1944 on special assignment at Wright Field in Dayton, Ohio, where she tested high altitude and low temperature equipment proposed for WASP use. This eventually led to her being a test pilot for some years after.

While on this assignment she found herself tapped to help design a relief tube for women.

Cockpits being designed for male use, items were not always suited to the WASP. One necessity on long runs was a relief tube for urinating. Women were unable to use the male equipment, so for cross-country travel they had a bucket in the back of the plane for such purposes. The prototype design for the women was constructed by attaching a baby oxygen mask to a tube that connected to the male relief tube. An official report described the device thusly:

> Relief tube is small bowl-shaped funnel that will fit in the palm of the hand and will thus be placed in position for use.

Source: *A WASP Among Eagles* by Ann Baumgartner Carl

They Flew the B-29

In the summer of 1944 Colonel Paul W. Tibbets, who later flew the *Enola Gay* over Hiroshima, recruited Dora Dougherty and

Dorothea Johnson Moorman to fly the B-29 bomber. Tibbets was responsible for training pilots on the Army Air Force's newest, biggest and most complicated bomber yet. His men were putting up unprecedented resistance to flying it, claiming it was unsafe and too big to manage.

DAS B-29 Enola Gay

The B-29 was the largest long-range bomber ever built. Rushed through production, it was critical to America's war with Japan. After Boeing's top pilot was killed testing it, the plane acquired a dangerous reputation. Tibbets was responsible for convincing pilots the B-29 was safe to fly. He believed that if he could train women to fly it successfully, he could convince men pilots that the huge aircraft was reliable. Neither Dougherty nor Moorman had ever flown a four-engine plane. Tibbets needed to prove that the B-29 could be flown by anyone – even women.

Dougherty said it was an easy airplane to fly. She was surprised when she sat at the controls, that it was so well engineered. She was impressed with the size of it; although it was a large plane, it was easier to fly than some of the twin-engine planes. On one of their flights Dougherty was in the air with Tibbets when an engine started smoking. Tibbets remarked: *Reacting with cool moves, she did everything just like the book said to do.*

TWU Ladybird Dougherty – Moorman –Tibbets

After gaining familiarity with the plane, Dougherty and Moorman flew it from Birmingham, Alabama to Alamogordo, New Mexico where it was christened *Ladybird*. Tibbets was ready to demonstrate their ability to fly it. He rounded up a group of male pilots who claimed the B-29 was unsafe and brought them on board. He was taking them for a ride, they believed, except they wondered what those women were doing in the cockpit. Tibbets told them the gals were flying it, which they did with ease.

Shortly thereafter, some internal publicity about their feat was distributed. An excerpt from Maintenance Bulletin No. 19 stated:

> Folks, those WASP that you see 'round about greased the "Ladybird" on No. 21 the other evening at 17:30 – and what a fine job mastering the mighty B-29 in just 8 hours transition with no previous time on four-engine aircraft. Is that good?

– Or are we a little backward?

The two luscious femmes go by the names of Dora Dougherty and Dorothea Moorman from the Proving Grounds at good old Sand Strip Eglin. Stop them and ask a few questions on how to handle the equipment. You will be surprised how much knowledge is stored behind all that beauty.

They are carrying out some tests on engine heat, and what have you. This is quite a big job for two delicate dishes of femininity. Perhaps they should take some of our supermen for a ride and show them how to get off the ground with speed dispatch at a low head temperature.

Signed by: Harry Shilling Major, Air Corps Director of Maintenance

The demonstration was a success. At least the men no longer objected to flying the B-29. But Air Staff Major General Barney Giles brought the demonstrations to an abrupt halt, telling Tibbets that the women were ...*putting the big football players to shame.* Giles was also worried that an accident would unleash tremendous adverse publicity. Dora and Dorothea were sent back to Eglin Field, Florida shortly after that, and never flew a B-29 again.

Years later, in a letter from Harry McKeown to Dora Dougherty Strother dated August 2, 1995, he reflected on the B-29 experience:

Dear Dr. Strother:

Before you throw this letter into the trash-basket, let me introduce myself. In 1944 I met you with Col. Tibbets and Didi Moorman when you brought a B-29 to Clovis AFB, Clovis, N.M. I was the Director of Maintenance & Supply and Base Test Pilot at the time. You came to show us that the B-29 plane was not one to be feared. You were the pilot that day and demonstrated your excellent flying skills and convinced us the B-29 was the plane that any pilot could be proud to fly. From that day on we never had a pilot who didn't want to fly the B-29.

It has been many years but I have never forgotten that day at Clovis and never will. I recently read about you in the Confederate Air Force "Dispatch" dated July/Aug. 1985, that a friend of mine had given me. I have asked the CAF to send this letter on to you and hope that you will receive it. I realize that it was a long time ago, but I still want to thank you for your helping me that day at Clovis. I will admit that I was scared, even though I had just returned from flying B-24s in North Africa. You made the difference in my flying from then on. I wasn't the only pilot that felt this way, and I am sure that they would thank you too if they knew where you were.

The article didn't mention Didi Moorman so I assume that she has passed on. She was the Co-pilot that day.

Thank you again and with kindest regards, I remain,

Harry McKeown Lt. Col. USAF (Ret.)

Teresa James and the P-47

Teresa James was one of the original WAFS pilots. She tells about being at a party one night when a male pilot kept trying to get her attention by regaling her with stories about how difficult it was to fly pursuit planes. Then he told her the old tale about going off to war tomorrow. She was not impressed, nor taken in.

The next day she was checking out her plane before mounting the wing when this same soldier spotted her. In disbelief he shouted: *What are you doing here?* She coolly climbed aboard, warmed up her engine for takeoff, and waved as he stood watching her head down the runway.

Teresa primarily flew ferrying missions. She was a highly skilled pilot as the planes the WASP ferried ranged from the primary and secondary trainers they had flown at Avenger Field to fast single-engine pursuit planes, fighter planes, two-engine and four-engine bombers, and two-engine cargo planes. The planes flown by the Ferrying Division were made by many manufacturers, which meant they had different equipment and controls, speeds, maneuverability, weight, altitude ranges, take-off and landing techniques and emergency procedures. But she and the other women proved themselves in mastering all the variables.

Teresa's P-47 Transition Flight

The WASP were getting established at Camp Davis during July, 1943. At about that same time Teresa was to begin P-47 transition at Wilmington, Delaware. Transition is the term that refers to the moment in training when a pilot moves up to a larger plane.

The P-47 Thunderbolt, known as the "Jug," was nicknamed because of its beefy look. It was reputed to be one of the most successful fighters in WWII. It had a big cockpit designed for robust guys, and many instruments to manage. The view from the cockpit was fine, considering that you had a big round engine in front of you. The P-47 looked ungainly, but among American WWII fighters, it was probably one of the more maneuver-

HWS Teresa James

able, and able to fly long distances with the bombers it escorted. The P-47 had wingtip gas tanks that could be dropped after use.

She gives a wonderful description of what it was like to solo in a P-47: I had just returned to the base, dog-tired after a long flight in a PT-19. Betty Gillies was sitting in the office. She handed me a copy of some tech orders. I was to check out in the P-47. *Whenever there's a P-47 on the flight line, go sit in it and get familiar with the operating and emergency procedures,* she said. I got all palsy-jawed when I heard that! Most of my flying time was in smaller aircraft.

So for several days I warmed the cockpit seat and studied everything I could about the "Jug" as it is affectionately called. I was scared to death of flying it. This was no trainer. The cockpit had only enough room for a single pilot - me - so my first flight was a solo.

I'd heard the guys discussing the flight characteristics of this seven-ton flying arsenal. Twenty-eight hundred horsepower! I had learned on something with about fifty. And the designer, something-or-other Kartvelli, armor plated the cockpit to protect the pilot from injury. I was happy to hear that - in case the engine quit on takeoff, you could plow through a building and only kill the people in front of you.

There was no forward visibility because of the huge engine. One of the guys said the real sweat was trying to keep the plane in the middle of the runway while taking off and landing. You had to look out at a forty-five-degree angle to keep the same spacing between the wing and edge of the runway.

As it turned out my mother and sister, Betty, came down to visit on the Fourth of July weekend only to find I was scheduled to fly my first P-47 on July 5. They warned me the day

HWS P-47 Thunderbolt (Jug)

before I was to fly it, so I had twenty-four hours to worry. And of course, Mom and Betty were there to see me being a total wreck. I later learned that while I was up, my mother disappeared to the base chapel to say the Rosary and beg God and the saints for her daughter's safe return to earth.

Anyway, the morning arrived too soon. I had butterflies in my stomach as I walked to Base Operations. I noticed a large crowd had gathered at the hangar near the P-47. There stood Captain Bing on the wing, waiting to give me a verbal checkout on preflight, cockpit and emergency procedures. Then, satisfied that I had done my homework, he wished me luck and told me to go up and practice stalls and spins. His parting shot: *After takeoff, you'll be twenty miles out past New Castle before you get the gear up.* What a confidence builder!

Well, my heart was in my mouth as I went through the thirty-two-item checklist before and after engine start. Satisfied that all the gauges were working, I closed the hatch, waved goodbye to Bing, released the brakes and slowly taxied - zigzagging back and forth on the taxi strip until I reached the active runway.

I sat for several minutes until a couple of aircraft taxied up behind me. I finally got up enough courage to call the tower and say I was ready for takeoff to which the operator replied: *Pull up into position and hold.*

I pulled onto the runway, made sure I was lined up in the middle, and locked the tail-wheel. Then I heard the soft male voice from the tower: *P-47 cleared for takeoff.*

I pushed the throttle to twenty-seven hundred RPM. The sudden power pushed me back against the seat as I rolled down the runway. I was off in nothing flat. I had the flaps and gear retracted as I passed over the end of the runway. That engine was purring like a kitten as I climbed to altitude over the practice area at eight thousand feet. I flew some basic maneuvers, shallow, medium and steep turns. The stalls unnerved me, but I was amazed at the clean recovery. My early flying instructor, Pete Goff, told me to always take an unfamiliar aircraft to high altitude and practice letdowns and landings at an imaginary airport in the sky. You can correct any mistake upstairs!

So I proceeded to land at Pete Goff's imaginary airport in the sky, mentally contacting the tower, reporting positions throughout maneuvering up to landing. I slowed the plane to make a downwind entry into the traffic pattern - speed 170 miles per hour. I dropped the gear and, wow, what a thud! Rocked the wings back and forth to ascertain that the gear was down and locked.

I continued to the make-believe base leg, dropped two inches of flaps at 150 miles per hour, prop to 2,350, continued to final approach, dropped full flaps, cowl closed. Glide at 135 mph to landing. OK, this works. Now all I had to do was get down all in one piece.

I started back toward the airport, called the tower when I was close, and was cleared downwind. I entered the traffic pattern just like I practiced upstairs, except this time was for real! Turning on base leg, my heart was racing while I kept my eyes focused on the landing area. Turning final, I got a *cleared to land* from the tower.

As I crossed the threshold of the field, I shifted my gaze to a forty-five-degree angle to the runway to keep the plane in the middle of it. I made a beautiful three-point landing. I really greased it! The tower operator congratulated me as I rolled to the end of the runway and on to Base Ops to great cheers. All these people were applauding. They were thinking, *She didn't kill herself!*

I did it! So, as it turns out, I found out the mystique was just a lot of male stories. The P-47 is a real pussycat, but with great claws and silky whiskers. What she's saying is: *Pet me gently!*

Source: *The Originals* by Sarah Byrn Rickman

Wichita, Kansas News Story

A common type of news story that appeared during the first months of WASP ferrying planes were small articles in local newspapers near the airbases. When they did appear, the major part of the article would elaborate on the attractive women rather than their extraordinary achievements. The Wichita Beacon gave this glowing account:

The daily routine of delivery of military airplanes to the armed forces was given the feminine touch Friday at the local Boeing plants, when a comely quartet of pilots of the Women's Auxiliary Squadron flew away four Boeing PT-17 Kaydet Primary Trainers.

Friday's flight was the first time the newly-organized WAFS have operated out of Wichita. Flight line mechanics, long used to daily contact with ferry pilots quickly broke into smiles and snapped into their duties when the able young ladies appeared. Hardened flight engineers scurried to help with luggage, and the colorful and expressive jargon of the flight hangar subsided into a good-natured bantering.

Source: *Clipped Wings* by Molly Merryman

A Strafing Incident

Katherine "Kaddy" Landry Steele and Nell Stevenson Bright were on a strafing mission early one morning. They were to strafe troops on the ground as a surprise maneuver. As the planes flew in low, the troops flattened themselves to the ground as they were trained to do. Then as the two WASP pulled up they spotted a lone jeep and strafed him. Instead of following protocol, the soldier simply waved. One of the women yelled: *That SOB just waved...let's go get him.* As they dived down he jumped from the moving jeep, pulled off his T-shirt in surrender waved it with vigor. Mission accomplished!

Caro Bayley Bosca, Several Remembrances...

Strafing Mission with A Twist

At Biggs Army Airfield, El Paso, Texas, Caro was on a strafing simulation mission. The antiaircraft gunners were to be prepared for strafing in real battle conditions. With the sun at her back, she put the "Dauntless" into a steep dive, aiming right for the infantry below. Nearly invisible against the high desert sun, she then pulled up at the last minute and streaked behind the recruits. With a broad grin and a chuckle, she saw the recruits turn their guns around long after she had started climbing for another pass.

When Caro gained altitude and began to dive for another simulation, the sergeant on the ground decided to let his boys have some fun. Word had gotten around that the pilot was a woman. As Caro came out of her dive no more than a hundred feet above the recruits, their greeting was unmistakable and she laughed out loud – she had just been mooned!

Source: *Saturday Evening Post* by John Bollow

We Are Gentlemen...

Caro Bayley was taxiing down the runway on a radar-tracking mission when she noticed that she was on a collision path with several B-24s. As she was deciding what to do, the tower controller said to the lead B-24: *Let the A-24 go first...you must be gentlemen.*

Ten WASP and Their B-25 Adventure

Caro Bayley recalled: In late 1943 our long cross country flight was to Douglas, Arizona in B-25s. We flew to Douglas, walked across the border, and each bought a gallon of something for our Christmas party at Mather Field. On the way back Mather notified us that the weather was turning bad at Sacramento, so we should land at Baker Field and await instructions. Five B-25s (10WASP and 5 Instructors) landed and parked the five planes smack in front of the operations office. We went to the hotel, and of course none of us had any money except Sammy, who was the daughter of Roy Chapin, who helped start the Hudson Company. Sammy bought a tube of toothpaste and we each paid her a dime for the evening and morning 2 squirts. We still laugh about that.

Next morning we 10 girls and our 5 instructors were in the operations office and a "chicken" Colonel came up to me and said, *Miss, what are you girls doing in my office.* I said (as softly as I could—knowing how fragile a "chicken" Colonel is), Sir, we brought those B-25s in last night because the weather was bad at Mather. He stomped over to the door, saw those B-25s, stepped over to the traffic desk and demanded: *Sergeant give me my clearance.* I watched him go out and climb into a BT-13, which unfortunately was parked right underneath one of our B-25's wings, and he steamed out through the rain puddles. He was mad and apparently jealous of girls flying a B-25 while he was stuck in a training plane. We got quite a chuckle out of it.

Caro Bayley's Comeuppance

Sometime later, I had my comeuppance. I had flown from Biggs Field, El Paso to Love Field in Dallas with a crew chief, to get an airplane part. It was good flying in a TB-26, a nice airplane. We went into maintenance, got the part, and started our engines. The tower asked me to hold for a P-38 that was going to taxi right in front of my parking spot. I gladly did so because one of my secret passions was to fly a P-38. I was going to get a good close look at it and I got my camera

DAS P-38 Lightning

ready. But I dropped my camera when I saw this gorgeous woman go by with her long blond hair flowing from a thrown back canopy. Then I understood why the "chicken" Colonel was so bent out of shape.

Years later, at the Dayton Air Show celebrating the Wright Brothers' 100 years of aviation, I invited a group of WASP to Springfield for a mini reunion. Betty Blake [the P-38 pilot] came to the gathering. We got along fine, but after all these years it took me a while to warm up to her. Now her once blonde hair is gray.

Lois Brooks

In May, 1944 the landing gear would not lock down on Lois' A-24.

The CO in the tower talked me through the procedures and I left the area to try some half snap rolls, or we called it a vertical reverse, to break the wheel loose. No luck. So the CO gave me permission to do a belly landing on the runway. [Just a week prior, a man had landed wheels up alongside the runway in sand and scooped sand packing it into the engine and plane – it was not flyable again.] I brought it in on its belly so gently that the only damage was the bent propeller. The maintenance crew had the plane flying the next day.

Later, Lois Brooks was given a Letter of Commendation for her skill in bringing her crippled plane in.

Sunny Exposure

WASP students loved the PT with its open cockpit, especially in the warm, sunny Texas weather at 3000 feet. Sally Van Wagenen Keil tells of a humorous event, in *Those Wonderful Women in their Flying Machines*:

One day a trainee was soloing on a perfect day and could not resist exposing herself to the sun. She soon learned that, although Cochran's Convent was off limits to male cadets, in the skies women trainees were fair game. She trimmed the PT perfectly so that it flew almost by itself, and held it straight and level by holding the stick still between her knees. Checking for other aircraft in the area and seeing none, she took her shirt off and leaned back, her face turned toward the sun. After several luxurious minutes, she heard an unexpected roar. Opening her eyes, she saw two other PTs on either side of her. Soon she was surrounded by a flock of primary trainers. In the cockpits were not women trainees from Avenger Field, but male cadets who were grinning and waving enthusiastically. Her PT began to weave and bob as she fumbled with her shirt in the windy cockpit. The shirt slipped out of her hands and sailed away over the Texas plains. Above the roar of the engines, her aerial audience cheered. She ducked down in the cockpit and, sneaking looks over the side, banked steeply and headed back toward Avenger Field. When she landed, she taxied to the flight line, cut the engine. From a seemingly empty cockpit, waiting trainees heard a voice yell: *Somebody bring me a blanket!*

Emma Coulter Ware and Widget

Adela Scharr met Emma Coulter during a ferrying trip from Long Beach. Arriving in El Paso, on June 6, 1944, "D Day," Adela was forced to delay the rest of her trip because of a huge thunderstorm that kept everyone grounded. This included Emma whose tow-target mission was cancelled. Emma offered Adela a spare bunk at their Biggs barracks for the night.

It was that night that Emma told the story about how the WASP at Biggs came to have a mascot named Widget, a Pomeranian. While at Liberty Field, Emma was on an assignment to Wright-Patterson in Dayton, Ohio, with a man named Tony. Tony had a small

Pomeranian that slept in his fleece lined flying boot, and Emma was really taken by this dog. On their way they stopped in Pittsburgh to visit her family. She told them about the dog and an aunt decided to get her a puppy. A friend who flew a Cub delivered the Pomeranian puppy to Emma at Liberty Field, Georgia.

From then on, Widget and Emma were inseparable. She was able to keep the dog since the WASP were civilians and she wasn't hassled much by the military. Widget became the women's mascot. He even got in some flying time. One day Emma, Widget and Lois Brooks started out for Reno, Nevada, Lois' childhood home, in an old Helldiver. Along the way they had to stop in Las Vegas. After landing, Emma noticed the flaps were still down and they would not retract. The air force mechanic reported that they would have to order a new worm gear from Sears in Dallas.

So the gals caught a bus to Reno. Emma always kept Widget hidden in her coat and Widget knew to keep quiet. In Reno they met another WASP and went to a local bar. Widget was along for the ride, of course, and she was in heat. The local lady bouncer had no idea Widget was in the bar, inside Emma's coat, and could not understand why she had to keep chasing all the male dogs out of the bar. Widget no doubt provided her WASP friends with many hours of affection and some good adventures.

Source: C. Andy Hailey – http://wwii-women-pilots.org

Amelia Earhart

I want to include something about Amelia Earhart because she had such a profound impact on most of these women. She inspired them to go for their dreams, and her spirit and vitality was often cited as reasons to commit themselves to flying.

Amelia Earhart disappeared in 1937 while attempting an around the world flight.

She was just shy of 40 years of age. In her short life she lived large, having ventured far beyond pilots male or female. She was a pioneer, a woman who wanted to break out of traditional roles, and a champion for equality. And she was a woman of enormous public acclaim, including the adoration of Eleanor Roosevelt.

DAS Amelia Earhart

She was the first woman to fly the North Atlantic to England – soloed in 1932. Her famous flight around the world started May 21, 1937 and she disappeared July 2, 1937 near Howland Island, just 7000 miles short of completion.

Amelia was a solitary woman, and she was happiest in the air. She had agreed, earlier, to accept her future husband's proposal of marriage. She wrote this letter to her husband to be:

> You must know again my reluctance to marry, my feeling that I shatter hereby chances in work which means so much to me…Please let us not interfere with the other's work or play, nor let the world see our private joys or disagreements. In this connection I may have to keep some place where I can go to be myself now and then, for I cannot guarantee to endure at all times the confinement of even an attractive cage…I must exact a cruel promise, and that is you will let me go in a year if we find no happiness together.

Source: *Amelia* by Jean L. Backus

Who Were These Women?

FOLLOWING ARE ALL the Camp Davis WASP biographies that were found:

Class	Name	WASP Name	Status
43.5	Ann Baumgartner Carl	Baumgartner	
43.3	Lois Brooks Hailey	Brooks	
43.4	Alta Corbett Thomas	Corbett	
43.3	Emma Coulter Ware	Coulter	
43.3	Marcia Courtney Bellassai	Courtney	
43.3	Betty Deuser Budde	Deuser	
43.3	Dora Dougherty Strother McKeown	Dougherty	
43.3	Marion Hanrahan	Hanrahan	Deceased
43.3	Lois Hollingsworth Ziler	Hollingsworth	Deceased
43.4	Dorothea Johnson Moorman	Johnson	Deceased
43.4	Martha Lawson Volkomener	Lawson	
43.3	Laurine Nielsen	Nielsen	Deceased
43.3	Mabel Rawlinson	Rawlinson	Killed
43.4	Frances Rohrer Sargent	Rohrer	
43.3	Joyce Sherwood Secciani	Sherwood	
43.4	Betty Taylor Wood	Taylor	Killed
43.4	Ruth Underwood Florey	Underwood	
43.4	Helen Wyatt Snapp	Snapp	

Ann Baumgartner Carl

When Ann Baumgartner Carl was born on August 27, 1918 in an Army hospital in Augusta, Georgia, her father was fighting in the Amiens region of France. As soon as they could travel, she and her mother moved to New Jersey to live with her grandparents. After the Armistice in France, her father returned and they moved to a small shingled bungalow in Plainfield, New Jersey where they would be within commuting distance of New York City.

TWU Ann Baumgartner Carl

After graduating from college Ann was still in a quandary as to what she wanted to do, and, hungry for adventure, decided to spend some time in Europe. Returning home, she was employed by Eastern Airlines where she decided her next adventure would be flying lessons. A little airport near Basking Ridge had a Civilian Pilot Training program that had ended. But an instructor volunteered to take her up in a Piper Cub and be her teacher. She thought: *This is what I was made for*.

She primarily flew small aircraft like the Piper Cub until earning her private pilot license. She eventually purchased half interest in a Piper Cub and set about reaching her next goal, building up the 200 flying hours required for a commercial pilot license. She also volunteered to fly for the Civil Air Patrol and flew patrol, search, and rescue missions during the first half of 1942.

Ann interviewed with Jackie Cochran in late 1942, and was accepted into the third WFTD class beginning on January 15, 1943. Unfortunately she caught the measles during training and, because of time missed while sick, completed her training with the fifth WASP Class 43.5 that graduated in September, 1943.

She worked through the rigors of training at Avenger Field, Sweetwater, Texas, enjoying all the challenges of escalating horsepower. Ann said: *In the streamlined PT-19 we could easily imagine we were flying fighters. It had responsive power with an upturn you could look straight down the wing to the ground. It was even hard to make a bad landing in it. And it would be the last airplane we flew with the wind in our face, an open cockpit. We flew long cross-country flights and in the moments of terror when we were not sure where we were over Texas, we had to clutch the chart so it wouldn't blow out of the cockpit.*

Her first assignment after graduation was tow target pilot at Camp Davis, North Carolina. Baumgartner and fellow WASP Betty Greene were chosen as replacement pilots for two WASP killed in flying accidents. Innocently, Ann and Betty walked into this hornet's nest believing that they were specially selected along with the others. But their first challenge was to be at home in a bare barracks room that had been occupied by two dead pilots.

After Camp Davis...

In February, 1944 Ann and Betty were transferred to Wright Field, Dayton, Ohio to test aero-medical equipment being designed for the WASP. It was described as testing high altitude equipment for WASP. But while that was in progress, they gave them another important assignment. Design a "relief tube" for women. Planes had only male equipment. They were to work with Brad Washburn, an expert in mountain expeditions, to decide on a proper design. A model would be made and they would test it themselves.

While all this was going on, Baumgartner and Greene became interested in what was going on with flight tests and discussed a possible assignment at Wright Field. Eventually Ann accepted a position in the transport and fighter test organization and was the first woman to fly a jet airplane on October 14, 1944. She continued as a test pilot and operations officer until the WASP program was ended in December, 1944.

When WASP deactivated, Ann married the designer of the P-82, Major William Carl. They had three children and Ann continued flight instruction and instrument training. She also wrote *A WASP Among Eagles* from which some of the above was derived.

Ann stated: *The WASP at Camp Davis faced difficulties and dangers with little help from Cochran and Washington or the commanding officer Stephenson, and they took upon themselves the task of protecting themselves as best they could, yet fulfilling their commitment as WASP. I felt honored to fly with them.*

Lois Brooks Hailey

Lois was born in Reno, Nevada on January 18, 1915. After graduating from the University of Nevada with a degree in Spanish and Education, she taught third grade. She wanted to teach band but women weren't allowed to do that, so she created and directed a band on her own. It was the only elementary school band in the state.

Lois recalled her initial interest in flying: *I started flying in 1939 after my brother twisted my arm. I was teaching elementary school in Minden, Nevada and was saving my money in hopes that I could go to*

CAH Lois Brooks Hailey

Julliard School of Music in New York City. After my brother got me in the air I was sold, and for three years my every penny went to flying.

In December, 1939 Lois, her cousin, and a friend purchased a new 65 horsepower Taylorcraft. In a month Lois soloed. She got her pilot's license the following April and after months of various recreational and acrobatic flying got her commercial license in 1941.

She kept flying as often as she could, and, having over 500 hours of flying, was invited by Nancy Love to join the WAFS. She didn't respond because she didn't want to go east. Also, she was more interested in meeting Jacqueline Cochran. Jackie Cochran's similar invitation appealed to her because it would likely be a western assignment. She set out on a weekend trip to meet Jackie Cochran at a recruitment meeting for the Womens Flying Training Detachment, WFTD. Telling them she was only there to meet Miss Cochran, she, nonetheless, agreed to take the physical. Besides, no need to worry, she probably wouldn't pass the exams because she had to wear glasses. The next thing she knew, however, Lois was getting gas rationing stamps and driving her 1936 Studebaker to Houston, Texas for flight training.

Lois said: *I was in Class 43.3 graduating in July, 1943 and we were assigned to four ferrying bases at Wilmington, Delaware; Dallas, Texas; Long Beach, California; and Romulus, Michigan. All had checked in at their new bases and hardly stayed one night before they had orders to report to Washington, DC. Here we re-convened at the Mayflower Hotel, and were whisked off to meet in the Pentagon office of General Henry "Hap" Arnold. He and Jackie Cochran explained that we would be an experimental group training for tow target work, and we would leave immediately for the Tow Target Squadron at Camp Davis, North Carolina. We were put through the high altitude chamber at Bolling Field to train us in oxygen mask use at high altitudes. We then boarded a DC-3 for the swamps of Camp Davis. The pilot had some trouble finding it. When we arrived, we marched to mess in our khakis with men whistling.*

After Camp Davis...

Lois transferred to Liberty Field, Georgia in the PQ-8 radio-controlled drone program in January, 1944 then later to Biggs Field, El Paso, Texas. In May, 1944 the landing gear would not lock down on her A-24. She recalled: *The CO in the tower talked me through the procedures and I left the area to try some half snap rolls, or we called it a vertical reverse, to break the wheel loose. No luck. So the CO gave me permission to do a belly landing on the runway. I brought it in so gently on*

CAH Lois Hailey – Later

its belly that the only damage was the bent propeller. The maintenance crew had the plane flying the next day. I was given a Letter of Commendation. [Just a week prior, a man had landed wheels up alongside the runway in sand and scooped sand packing it into the engine and plane – it was not fly-able again.]

Lois remained at Biggs until the WASP function was ended in December, 1944. After WASP was disbanded, she became a certified flight instructor and stayed in El Paso.

There, she met and soloed her future husband in 1947. She also instructed and soloed her father, Charles Brooks, in 1947. She married, went back to teaching, and eventually raised a son as a single mom. Retiring at 65, she has survived four battles with cancer, but still maintains her interest in the WASP.

Alta Corbett Thomas

Alta was born on May 25, 1918 in Portland, Oregon. Her early life revolved around horses. Her parents believed there was more to life than horses and sent her off to college. After college she hung out at Swan Island Airport in Willamette River and learned to fly.

She was working in the Pentagon for Air Branch G-2 when the WASP program started. The War Department had to release Alta so she could

ACT Alta Corbett Thomas

be hired to the Civil Service Program as a WASP, and, once accepted, she was trained with Class 43.4. She was assigned to Tow Target Squadrons, 1st and 3rd, at Camp Davis, North Carolina and at Liberty Field, Georgia.

Alta remembers: *Our missions were high and low tows, Identification Friend or Foe-IFF, and on occasion flying an officer cross-country to Orlando, Baltimore, and other bases. We flew the A-24, B-34, and UC-78, for night searchlights, and the AT-7 and AT-11 for cross-country and instrument training. Many of the planes, especially at Camp Davis, were a far cry from factory fresh. Consequently we had a high regard for our ground crews.*

Alta was administrator on squadron matters, doing the needed record keeping and assuming the role of "house mother," as some recall. It is said that this gentle woman was tenacious about seeing that the women in her squadron were treated well.

After Camp Davis...
Alta transferred to Liberty Field in March, 1944.

After deactivation, Alta wrote every aircraft company to no avail. Pilots were plentiful with the war in Europe winding down, and she was not needed. However, the CAA recruited trainees to take over air, ground, and weather communications in Alaska. This appealed to her. She reported to Boeing Field for training and was pleasantly surprised to find three other WASP there, too. Her first assignment was shared with Laurine Nielsen. At Gustavus, a new auxiliary airfield for Juneau, Alaska, there were three communicators, each standing an eight hour watch. It was at Gustavus that Alta met Ralph Thomas and sometime later they were married.

ACT Alta Corbett Thomas – Later

Emma Coulter Ware

Emma was born in Greensburg, Pennsylvania in 1915. She was an only child and spent much of her youth interested in horses and dogs. Both her father and grandfather were generals, and both rode horses as their main mode of transportation in the service. She eventually got her pilot license and owned her own plane.

When Emma heard about Jackie Cochran's program for women pilots, she flew to Houston to join. She flew her own plane, which was nicknamed Private Willis, a character in a Gilbert and Sullivan musical. After completing basic training in Class 43.3, she was sent to Romulus Army Air Base, Romulus,

CAH Emma Coulter Ware

Michigan along with Lois Brooks. Both Emma and Lois were only there for a short time when Jackie Cochran ordered them to Washington, DC where they met General Hap Arnold. While in DC they reconnected with Lois Hollingsworth and Betty Budde, also from Class 43.3, and all were told of their new duties. From there the four were sent to Camp Davis, North Carolina where they were joined by Kay Menges, another WASP from Class 43.3. At Camp Davis they were trained to fly tow targets using old modified war-spent Navy bombers.

After Camp Davis...

Later, Emma and the others trained at Liberty Field, Georgia with radio-controlled planes. After completing tow and radio-controlled target training, all five women were sent to Biggs Field, Texas where they flew and helped train troops for war until the WASP were disbanded in December, 1944. They were the first WASP to arrive at Biggs.

While at Biggs, Emma met and became engaged to Major James B. Ware. As the WASP were having their farewell celebration on December 19, 1944, she and the Major were wed. Emma and James settled in St. Louis, Missouri and raised six children.

Marcia Courtney Bellassai

Marcia E. Courtney Bellassai was born in Hartford, Wisconsin on March 5, 1919. She graduated from Hartford High School in 1936.

CAH Marcia Courtney Bellassai

Like many of the WASP, Marcia joined the Civilian Pilot Training program while working to get her BA. She obtained her CPT training at the University of Wisconsin and got her private license in 1940. She had completed the primary training in an Aeroncas and then acrobatics in a Waco biplane. She was about to start her instructor training when women were forced out of the program because of the demand for male instructors. She was able to use some of her ground school training to complete her Political Science degree in 1942.

From spring of 1941 to December of 1942, Marcia worked for Piper Aircraft Corporation ferrying Cubs around the country, including deliveries to Texas and an Army glider school in South Dakota. During this time she also joined the Piper Civil Air Patrol Squadron and, looking smart in her CAP uniform, appeared in an advertisement for the Elgin Watch company.

In December, 1942 Marcia joined the WASP along with Lois Brooks, Lois Hollingsworth, Betty Deuser, Emma Coulter, Mabel Rawlinson, Joyce Sherwood and others in Class 43.3. After basic training was completed in Sweetwater, Texas, she was sent briefly to Romulus, Michigan and then to the Tow Target Squadron at Camp Davis, North Carolina. She flew antiaircraft artillery missions in the AT-6, A-24, A-25, and B-34.

Marcia and Mabel Rawlinson were close friends. In fact, they had been to Mexico together just before transferring to Camp Davis. Mabel was killed in a plane crash. Marcia and others were in the barracks, heard her plane in trouble, looked out and saw it crash. When asked how hard it was to keep going after this happened, she said: *We were all affected deeply by it, and as I recall it, two resigned.*

Marcia and Florence Knight were the first to qualify in the larger B-34.

After Camp Davis...

In January, 1944 Marcia was transferred to Liberty Field, Georgia where she continued to fly the B-34 for tow target practice. Lois, Holly, Betty, and Emma were sent to Biggs Army Air Field in El Paso, Texas.

After the WASP were deactivated in December, 1944, Marcia accepted a job as an aircraft accident analyst for the Air Safety Division of the Air Transport Command in Gravelly Point, Virginia. From there she worked for the Joint Attaché Office, U.S. Legation, in Bucharest, Rumania analyzing and reporting on economic intelligence. She traveled broadly throughout Europe and her last flight was as co-pilot on a C-46 going from Rome to Paris. While in Rumania, she met Anthony Bellassai, a member of the U.S. Signal Corps. They married and raised 5 children.

Betty Deuser Budde

Betty was born on August 15, 1920 in Alameda, California. Soon after, her family moved to Oakland, California near Oakland Airport. Her father often took the family to the airport for various events and she developed an interest in flying.

In 1937 Betty graduated from high school and went to work as a private secretary in Oakland. In 1941 she applied to the Civilian Pilot Training program - CPT where she earned her private pilot license. Her training was paid for by a scholarship she won in a competition sponsored by the Oakland Chamber of Commerce. After the

CAH Betty Deuser Budde

bombing of Pearl Harbor, her flying had to be moved to high in the mountains of Plumas National Forest as flying near the Pacific shore was prohibited.

She accumulated 75 hours of flying time and after hearing of Jacqueline Cochran's women's flying program she wrote for information. Her reply was a request to head for training in Houston, Texas.

Betty joined the 3rd class, 43.3, which included Lois Hollingsworth, Lois Brooks, Emma Coulter, Dora Dougherty, and 43 others; training started in January, 1943. While in Houston they learned to fly Taylorcraft, Cub Aeronca, PT-19s, BT-13s, BT-15s, and UC-78s. They then moved to Sweetwater, Texas to complete their training.

Just before graduation Jacqueline Cochran was in Sweetwater with a reporter and photographer from LIFE magazine. Betty, Jackie, and others were captured on a half page picture on page 74 of the July 19, 1943 issue.

After she got her wings on July 3, 1943, Betty's first assignment was as a ferry pilot at Love Field, Dallas, Texas. She was only there a few days when she, along with others, was called to Washing-

BDB Betty Deuser Budde – Later

ton, DC to meet with Jackie Cochran and General Hap Arnold. Here they found out that they were not going to be ferrying new planes. The program was being expanded to use them for other tasks. By the end of July, 1943 they were reassigned to Camp Davis, North Carolina, flying tow targets for antiaircraft troop training.

After Camp Davis...

In September, 1943, Betty began training in the PQ-8 secret radio-control program. The PQs were used for targets and the WASP learned to fly them remotely. By October Betty and fourteen others were relocated to Liberty Field, Hinesville, Georgia for further training. Along with training on the PQ-8, Betty also logged time with the A-24 Douglas Dive Bomber, A-25 Curtiss Helldiver, B-34 Lockheed bomber and various Beechcraft ATs. Eventually she, along with others, was sent to Biggs Field, El Paso, Texas in January, 1944 and did various PQ and target towing duties until the WASPs were disbanded in December, 1944.

In January, 1944 Betty married Sergeant Fred Budde, and in the summer of 1945 they moved to Victorville, California and raised a family.

Betty's letters home give us insight into WASP life in another chapter.

Dora Dougherty Strother McKeown

Native of St. Paul, Minnesota, she was born November 23, 1920. Dora earned her wings in Class 43.3 and, after her WASP assignment, served later in a U.S. Air Force career that included aviation psychologist, human factors engineering, pilot and military officer.

Her flight accomplishments include two world flight records for rotorcraft. A resident of Ft. Worth, Texas, she was inducted into the Texas Women's Hall of Fame in 1987. She was also inducted into the U.S. Air Force Gathering of Eagles.

CAH Dora Dougherty
Strother McKeown

In the 1920s five year old Dora was enchanted by airplanes that flew over her home. For years she and her family trekked every Sunday afternoon after church to the airport to watch the planes take off and land. Her heroes at that time were not movie stars, rather aviators who were pushing back technology and doing fantastic things as pioneers. When she became a WASP, she was to become a pioneer herself.

After her first year at Cottey College in Nevada, Missouri, Dora heard about the Civilian Pilot Training program and applied. Only 10 percent of the applicants were to be women and she was happily accepted.

Dora was hooked from the beginning. She said: *I think that a lot of the excitement for me was that it's something new, that you're in control and that the success of the flight depends on you.* After the summer of training she was ready to fly. In her second year at Cottey, she used her allowance to gain more flying time to raise her rating.

An article in the *Chicago Tribune* describing a new Army program that would train women to ferry aircraft caught her eye. She replied and soon received her orders on January 15, 1943. She ended up at Avenger Field, Sweetwater, Texas. The regimen was tough with hard physical exercise, hours of ground school, and many hours of flight training. Dora recalled: *The army way of flying was different than civilian flight. The stall sequences were different and there were different maneuvers and ways military aircraft react than do civilian aircraft. So even coming in with a pilot's license didn't mean we were ready to fly military aircraft.*

After six months of training, she and her qualifying classmates received their wings on July 4, 1943. Her assignment was to Camp Davis, North Carolina for towing targets. Dora flew everything from L-4s through nearly all the military aircraft, with the unique experience of flying a B-29. Her sense of mission was aptly put: *It's difficult in these days to realize the mindset we all had. The country was at war, submarines were seen at our coasts. We were all motivated to do whatever we could to further the effort for peace, for our country to win the war.*

After Camp Davis...

In January, 1944 Dora and others in her group were sent to a restricted base at Liberty Field, Georgia where they were trained to fly remote-control drone aircraft. These teams of drone flyers became a tight-knit group with lasting bonds. Some of them were assigned later to Eglin Field, Florida.

Later in 1944, Lt. Col. Paul W. Tibbets, the pilot who flew the *Enola Gay* over Hiroshima, recruited Dougherty and Dorothea Johnson Moorman to learn to fly the B-29 bomber. Tibbets was responsible for training pilots on the Army Air Forces' newest, biggest and most complicated bomber yet. His men were putting up unprecedented resistance to flying it claiming it was unsafe and too big to manage.

Dougherty and Moorman only received three days of training, but they were successful in demonstrating that they could fly the giant plane. But Air Staff Major General Barney Giles stopped the program out of out of concerns for the risks taken. Dora and Dorothea were sent back to Eglin field, Florida and never flew a B-29 again. The story is told in more complete form in the WASP Stories chapter.

TWU Ladybird Dougherty – Moorman –Tibbets

As the WASP program was disbanded in December, 1944, Dora decided to return to Northwestern University. Flying still her passion, she then became an instructor and worked at the University of Illinois' aviation psychology lab in a program sponsored by the Navy. She went on to earn a master's degree there in applied psychology, and a doctorate in aviation education and psychology at New York University. She then worked for years as a human factors engineer for Bell Helicopter until her retirement.

When WASP were offered commissions, she accepted and remained in the Air Force Reserve retiring as a Lt. Colonel.

Dora Dougherty Strother McKeown sums up her view of her WASP experience: *It was a magnificent opportunity. I think that aside from the thrill of it, anytime that any of the women pilots flew anyplace, they felt they were representing women worldwide and for generations to come. We knew we were breaking barriers, and we had to fly our best.*

Marion Hanrahan

Marion was born in San Francisco, California. Her mother was one of the first American women to have a commercial pilot's license for single-engine planes in the 1930s. So Marion was fascinated by flight very early in her life. In 1935 when she was fourteen, she would cut high school classes and head out to Bendix Field. She earned her flying lessons by patching airplane wings. The flying community was so small that the world's most famous woman aviator, Amelia Earhart, a frequent visitor to Bendix Field, would sit leisurely giving the teenager flying tips.

CAH Marion Hanrahan

During the Lindbergh era when flying was rare among most Americans, Marion Hanrahan's contemporaries, smitten by the flying bug, were daring and lucky to get into flying. And most were so determined that one could not keep them away from it. After her Sweetwater training in Class 43.3, she was assigned to a ferrying squadron.

Marion was sent on a temporary basis from the Fifth Ferrying Group at Love Field to tow targets at Camp Davis for antiaircraft training. She said: *When we arrived we found that the A-24s had been returned from the South Pacific because they were no longer fit for combat. Their tires were worn and weak, the instruments were malfunctioning and the planes were in very sorry shape. There were even some indications of sabotage that were thought to be the result of resentment on the part of male pilots.*

After Camp Davis...

Marion Hanrahan decided she had enough. She loved airplanes and flying for too long to sour a lifelong enthusiasm. Being a target at Camp Davis and forced to fly weary airplanes, Marion decided that this is not the way she wanted to serve her country. She wrote Jacqueline Cochran a letter of resignation. Cochran replied with a rejection of her resignation. She then went to her old prior organization, the Air Transport Command Ferrying Division, who had released her for temporary duty at Camp Davis. Cochran blocked that request. Then Cochran finally relented allowing a resignation. Marion's experience was too valuable to lose from air assignments.

Marion Hanrahan immediately joined the WAVEs. Sent to Honolulu, she worked in the control tower, taught Navy cadets as a Link instructor, and flew as crew in DC-5s transporting admirals and USO celebrities to the liberated islands of the Pacific.

Lois Hollingsworth Ziler

Lois Hollingsworth was known as Holly. She was born in Tulsa, Oklahoma on October 14, 1920 and grew up in University City, Missouri. She has a vivid memory of Lindbergh's flight and the suspense from the time he took off until they got the word that he had landed. She was always interested in flight, and built kites and model airplanes from about age eight. Her father was an engineer and draftsman, and he helped her in that interest. But it was Lindbergh who inspired her to fly.

Lois lived her pre-adult years with her sisters, after both of her parents died. By age 14 she had purchased a horse with babysitting money. By age 16 she had soloed in an open cockpit biplane, and the following year she earned her private license.

CAH Lois Hollingsworth Ziler

While in high school she met Amelia Earhart, who was then a counselor at Purdue University. Earhart encouraged her to study engineering and she graduated with a degree in Mechanical Engineering with an option in Aeronautics. She then went to work for United Aircraft in Hartford, Connecticut. She was working toward a commercial pilot's license and planned to join the Civil Air Patrol.

When she saw an advertisement in the paper about flight training for military planes, Lois applied. She was notified to report for an interview in New York City. A 60 mile train ride later, she was interviewed by Jacqueline Cochran and she recalled: *I was really impressed by this striking woman and I wondered if what I wore was sufficient. My biggest worry was that I could not see without glasses. But it didn't seem to matter, as I was accepted.* Since she was in a critical occupation having to do with airplane design, her boss finally signed the required exemption after she pleaded that she wanted to do this.

Lois was then directed to report to Houston, Texas, in January of 1943. After a long hard train ride from Connecticut to Texas, she and several other young women arrived at Houston. There she became a trainee in the Women's Flying Training Detachment, which became WASP Class 43.3.

After completion of WASP training, Lois was sent to Dallas, Texas to the ferry command there. Then she was assigned to Romulus Army Air Base in Michigan as a ferrying pilot.

After a short assignment there, Lois was directed to report to Washington, DC where Cochran and General Hap Arnold met with her and other WASP at the Pentagon. General Arnold impressed them with his vision of the future for women pilots and described their mission, towing targets for antiaircraft artillery training. Could they do that? The women responded confidently: *We are young and can do anything.* They were taken through high-altitude testing there, and then loaded into a DC-3 and flown to Camp Davis, North Carolina.

After Camp Davis…

Lois and fourteen other WASP were sent to Liberty Field, Georgia in October, 1943 for additional training in radio-control. They returned after Christmas in Savannah, Georgia to Camp Davis and orders for them to go to three different air bases. Lois Hailey, Lois Hollingsworth, Betty Deuser, Kay Menges and Emma Coulter went to El Paso, Texas.

[There is a chapter on radio-controlled missions with more on this.]

After the WASP were disbanded in December, 1944, Holly became a certified flight instructor in El Paso, Texas, and earned a living teaching flying to GIs with GI Bill benefits. She married one of her students, Doyle Ziler, in 1946. A few years later she and Doyle moved to Dell City where they grew cotton and vegetables, raised chickens, cows, and pigs, and three children. She also obtained her teaching certificate and taught high school mathematics. She renewed her flight instructor rating, bought a Cessna 150, and started a flying school…a flight instructor again.

Dorothea Johnson Moorman

Dorothea "Didi" Johnson Moorman was born in 1919. Her early life was spent in Fort Dodge, Iowa. She learned to fly in nearby North Platte, Nebraska. When the War Department asked for women pilots to volunteer for the Army Air Corps, Didi answered the call. She left for training in February, 1943 and became part of the first class entering training in the Army Air Force Flying Training Detachment at Avenger Field in Sweetwater, Texas. Her class was designated 43.4.

Her first military assignment was to Camp Davis, North Carolina to

TWU Dorothea Johnson Moorman

the Tow Target Squadron. It was there she met and fell in love with a handsome and dashing pilot, Hank Moorman. They were married on New Year's Day, 1944.

After Camp Davis...

They were soon parted when, in January, she was transferred to Liberty Field, Georgia to be trained in a highly classified program to fly radio-controlled drone aircraft. Successfully completing that program, she was sent to Camp Edwards, Cape Cod, Massachusetts to the Tow Target Squadron to serve as a radio-control and tow target pilot.

Didi was then transferred to the Air Forces Proving Ground Command, Eglin Field, Florida. Here her assignment was to be the same as that at Camp Edwards, but she was soon tagged by Colonel Paul Tibbets to be one of two women to check out and demonstrate the new bomber, Boeing's B-29 Superfortress. Along with Dora Dougherty, she checked out after only three days of flight instruction from Colonel Tibbets. A B-29 assigned to them and named by Colonel Tibbets *The Ladybird*, served as a demonstration

TWU Tibbets – B-29 Strothers & Moorman

plane to prove that it was so easy to fly "that even a woman could fly it."

She returned to her new civilian life as Mrs. Henry Moorman, eventually settled in Big Pine Key, Florida and raised five children. Didi died in 2005.

Martha Lawson Volkomener

Martha's first impression about flying was not Charles Lindbergh…it was a pilot, earlier than Lindbergh, who came through town as a celebrity. Martha doesn't recall who it was, but as an 8 year old she was sufficiently struck by the idea of flying that she said: *Daddy, I'm going to fly airplanes when I grow up.* And that she did.

Marty, as she was known, learned to fly sea planes at the Kanawha Flying School near Charleston, South Carolina. She used her lunch breaks at work to pursue her dream of becoming a pilot. She recalled: *I could go fly for a half an hour at lunch and eventually logged about 80 hours flight time.*

MLV Martha Lawson
Volkomener – 1944

Her flying school knew of the WASP program and contacted them for information. Martha was asked if she would be interested: *Well, I just couldn't get there fast enough.* That was the beginning of a journey that lasted just over a year. But it was the fulfillment of her dreams.

She was in Class 43.4, training to fly military aircraft with the WASP at Avenger Field, Sweetwater, Texas. The military planes were different from her sea plane experience and she had to learn to fly all over again to graduate. All the women knew that they would have a flight check by a military officer, and it meant hard preparation. The officers washed out a lot of candidates. But she earned her wings and went on to experimental flying experiences.

Many WASP ferried planes from place to place. Martha flew anti-aircraft target tracking, towing a sleeve on a cable behind the airplane.

MLV Marty Early Flying

Marty recalled: *Cochran pushed us hard, but she was fair. She used to tell us over and over, you don't make any mistakes or it goes against the whole organization. And mistakes were not going to be made by this new recruit.*

After Camp Davis...

Marty was always asked to fly the lead in formations as the other pilots appreciated the fact that she would tell them the moves she was going to make well in advance. She said she did this for her own protection as well. She flew twin engine planes when doing bombing run exercises. She also flew many radio trailing missions so the ground crew could learn to track planes... mostly done at night. In her last months at Camp Davis, she participated in another experiment. The WASP were flying PQ-8 radio-controlled drones as target

MLV Marty Lawson Volkomener

planes, making the targets more realistic than the sleeve targets. [There is more on radio-controlled drones in another chapter]

She said: *I was at Camp Davis for about 8 months and it was the time of my life.*

When the WASP were disbanded in December, 1944, she didn't quit flying. Martha went to work for the Civil Aeronautics Administration as an aircraft communicator in Dillon, Montana. The CAA was the beginning of what is now the Federal Aviation Administration. She soon met the man she would marry and left flying to raise a family.

When you talk with Martha, she is quite modest about what she did as WASP, so she tempers some of her exciting times with a quiet demeanor. Marty is proud that she never had an accident, and that she never got lost on a cross country mission.

Laurine Nielsen

Laurine, known as Rene, was born on May 6, 1921, in Laurel, Nebraska. She was raised in Spearfish, South Dakota. Rene barnstormed with Clyde Ice and served in the WASP program, training in Class 43.3.

She was first stationed at New Castle Army Air Base, Wilmington, Delaware, then at Camp Davis. She ferried planes including the B-17, and towed aerial gunnery targets for both ground and aerial target practice. She kept a daily log from which excerpts are presented in another chapter.

After Camp Davis...
After deactivation of WASP in December, 1944, she and a friend home-

CAH Laurine Rene Nielsen

steaded and built a cabin on Ida Lake in Alaska. Eventually Rene founded the Palmer Flying Club. She instructed and flew throughout Alaska for the next 20 years. Rene died in 1988.

Mabel Rawlinson

Mabel was born March 19, 1917 in Greenwood, Delaware. She moved to Kalamazoo, Michigan to live with her aunt and attended college. Graduating with a BA degree in 1939 from Western Michigan University, Mabel worked at the Kalamazoo Public Library. In

1940 she started flying lessons and returned to Western Michigan University to take post-graduate civilian pilot training. She soloed on October 31, 1939 and received her private pilot's license. By then she was co-owner of an Aeronica Chief airplane. After the bombing of Pearl Harbor, the Civil Air Patrol was formed in Kalamazoo. She was flying every weekend and proudly wearing the uniform of the Civil Air Patrol.

CAH Mabel Rawlinson

Mabel reported on January 15, 1943 to Avenger Field in Sweetwater, Texas for her Army Air Force Pilot Training, Class 43.3. She transferred to Camp Davis after graduating and her assignment was towing targets for antiaircraft gunner training. Just one month later, while on a night flight with her instructor, her plane developed mechanical problems and crashed into pine trees near the runway. Her instructor survived, but Mabel was unable to escape the plane and died in the crash.

No compensation was available to the Rawlinson family because WASP were considered volunteer civilian pilots, not military. Transportation of her body and funeral expenses were borne by the Rawlinson family, with assistance from fellow WASP contributions. Mabel Rawlinson was honored with an American flag draped over her casket, and the Kalamazoo Civil Air Patrol honored her with buglers, fly-overs and solemn gun salutes.

Frances Rohrer Sargent

Fran was born July 24, 1919 and grew up in Atlanta, Georgia. After two years in the University of Georgia, she fell in love with flying. On a trip by air to Birmingham, Alabama with a friend, she decided that she wanted to fly: *When I got home, I went to the airport and found that a Delta pilot would teach me to fly. He took me on as a student and there was a place that rented airplanes. In the afternoons after work, I'd ride the streetcar out near the airport, a short walk and I'd take a flying lesson. I did all my flying late in the afternoons when there was still daylight, and sometimes on the weekend, and after that we'd have ground school.*

TWU Frances Rohrer Sargent

The Navy opened an air base in Atlanta to train instrument flight instructors. The war was getting closer and they were hiring. The Navy advertised for women who had flight experience and she got the job.

They hired about twenty women. They were trained for about a month and obtained instrument rating. This was so they could operate the simulators for instrument training. Jackie Cochran came to interview pilots and with her experience and training, Fran was hired into the WASP program. She said: *I believe that I had something exceptional to offer since I had instrument training and this is really important to all-weather flying.*

Fran was 24 years of age when she entered Class 43.4 at Sweetwater, Texas and she had her wings by August, 1943. Sweetwater was a small, remote town without much to do. Fran recalled: *We made a sport of diving our airplanes to run the buffalo. The rancher who owned the buffalo invited us all to a barbecue and held a rodeo for us. After that we decided not to do it any more.*

Fran's voyage from Sweetwater took her home to Atlanta briefly, then to Dallas, and finally by plane to Washington, DC. She recalls: *In Washington, we were tested in a high-altitude chamber, a test for high-altitude flying, and we were transported by train to Camp Davis, North Carolina. Only then did we know where we were being sent. Helen Snapp and I were in the last car of that train. Another train rammed us, and the front end and cowcatcher of that train was in our car. Fortunately, nobody was seriously hurt because all the suitcases had been stacked at the back end at the restroom and it cushioned the blow.*

When they arrived at Camp Davis, the word reached the women that a WASP had just crashed and sabotage was suspected. There was much speculation about whether jealous male pilots defending their turf could have put sugar in the gas tank. [Reports later disproved the theory of sabotage.]

After Camp Davis...
Fran married Floyd Sargent, a serviceman from Camp Davis, on May 14, 1944 after resigning from WASP, and was able to live in Wilmington, North Carolina while he finished out his military service. They settled in Savannah, Georgia, and later moved to Deming, New Mexico. After three children and a move to Florida, she re-involved herself in flying. She trained pilots for their licenses including instrument flying for 25 years at Miami - Dade Community College, one of the largest pilot training education sites in the country.

In 1996 Fran was presented the prestigious Greater Miami Aviation Association Annual Wright Brothers Award. Fran is justifiably proud of becoming an "Honorary Tailhooker" on March 13, 1972, when she survived an arrested carrier landing aboard the USS Lexington.

She still instructs and flies with pilots to meet their periodic checkout requirements. She also flies for her own pleasure and says: *I have had the good fortune to be able to work at something I love all my life.*

DAS Frances Rohrer Sargent – 2005

Joyce Sherwood Secciani

Joyce had wanted to fly as long as she could remember. She was born in San Diego, California. All her school years were in El Centro, and upon graduating from high school she signed up for the government sponsored Civilian Pilot Training program at Central Junior College.

Serious about dedicating herself to flying, she sold her beloved horse and stopped studying piano so she could devote all her energies to it. After earning her private license, she joined a flying club of 10 members and shared a 65 hp Interstate plane. After the attack at Pearl Harbor, private flying was not allowed within 200 miles of the U.S. coast. So Joyce helped another member of the club remove the wings of their plane, secure them, and transport it to Arizona so they could continue to fly.

CAH Joyce Sherwood Secciani

As soon as she heard about Jacqueline Cochran's program in January, 1943, she applied for it. 22 years old, Joyce was accepted and she headed for Houston, Texas where the training program began. There were no military quarters, so the women lived in a motor court. On May 16, 1943 they were transferred to Avenger Field, Sweetwater, Texas.

After graduating in July, 1943 Joyce and several classmates were sent to New Castle Army Air Base, Wilmington, Delaware. They were not there long enough to start flying, when she received orders to report to General Hap Arnold's office in Washington, DC along with 24 other WASP. After a few days of orientation and training, the group was reassigned to Camp Davis, North Carolina as part of the Tow Target Squadron near Wilmington, North Carolina.

Just two days after her friend Mabel Rawlinson was killed, Joyce also had engine failure in an A-24. According to the Army accident report, Joyce and the instructor managed a belly landing, the engine detached from the rest of the plane, the plane caught fire after stopping, and both Joyce and her instructor suffered minor injuries but no burns.

After Camp Davis...

In January, 1944 Joyce and several others were transferred to Liberty Field, Georgia. They trained and flew missions with radio-controlled targets. The targets were modified Culver Kaydets, PQ-8s and PQ-14s which were controlled from the co-pilot seat of a UC-78 or AT-11. They also flew administrative flights taking personnel or equipment from one base to another.

In April, 1944 Joyce and other WASP were ordered to the March Army Air Base in Riverside, California. At March, there were about 40 WASP pilots in the Tow-Target Squadron. They supported artillery training and radio-controlled target planes at several California locations. Some of her flights were from Van Nuys, California where she flew 100 miles out to sea to support radar tracking missions. While flying in southern California, Joyce also checked out in a P-63 King Cobra. It was then that she met Staff Sergeant Mario Secciani, who maintained these and other fighter planes. As a fighter, the P-63 was a single seat, so after studying the aircraft manual and getting some advice, Joyce took off on her own and had the thrill of flying that beautiful aircraft.

After the WASP were disbanded on December 20, 1944, Joyce was sad to leave, but proud to have served with this great group of women pilots. In memory of this service, she designed and carved from wood a 6-7 inch tall statue of a WASP returning from her last long mission. She is in her flight suit with goggles, map in hand, and a parachute slung over her shoulder. The pedestal bears the inscription "Mission Completed." Later in life, Joyce learned how to cast bronze copies of the carving. She has given most of them away and is holding the last three for her grandchildren.

DAS Joyce Sherwood Secciani Carving

Joyce got her civilian pilot ratings for single and multi-engine planes and for commercial and instrument flying. In 1945 she and Mario got married and she found a job with Flabob Flying Service at a small airport in Riverside where she flew charter flights, checked out returning military pilots transitioning from fighters and bombers to light civilian planes.

Joyce and her husband Mario ultimately settled in El Cajon, California, built a house and raised two children. She helped set up WASP exhibits at the San Diego Aerospace Museum.

Betty Taylor Wood

Betty was born in New Berlin, Illinois in March, 1921. She graduated from Sierra Junior College in Auburn, California. She was living in Auburn when she joined the WASP and reported for pilot training at Sweetwater, Texas.

TWU Betty Taylor Wood

On the day Betty graduated from her basic training, Class 43.4, she married a WASP instructor, "Shorty" Wood. She then went to her assignment at Camp Davis, North Carolina for tow target training. Betty's plane crashed on September 23, 1943, killing her and the chaplain who was flying with her. She had not been in the WASP program for long. The A-24s being used for tow target training were worn out from war duty, not well maintained due to lack of parts, and being run on lower octane fuel than they required. Sugar found in the fuel tank was also suspected to be the cause. There were many possible contributing factors. [More information on the investigation is presented in the chapter on crashes.]

Ruth Underwood Florey

Ruth is a native Texan, born in Brownwood in 1922. While she was attending Daniel Baker College she took advantage of a Government sponsored Civilian Pilot Training program, and earned her private pilot's license.

When Pearl Harbor was attacked, the men in Ruth's family enlisted. Her husband joined the Army Air Corps, and her brother was training to fly B-25s. Ruth thought about joining a typing pool to help the war effort. Then a surprise letter from Jackie Cochran, Director of the Women's Flying Training Detachment, asked if she would train to become a pilot: *I couldn't believe it and I jumped at the chance.*

TWU Ruth Underwood Florey

She reported to Carswell Air Force Base for her physical. She said: *It was nerve-wracking. My blood pressure was out the window from stress. Here I was... a girl from the country...with 5,000 men, male doctors and male nurses, they didn't know about the WASP program. They didn't know what to do with me. They thought it was a big joke.* She passed, however, and was off to Sweetwater, Texas for six months of training in the hot summer months of 1943.

After graduating from Class 43.4, Ruth reported to Camp Davis, North Carolina and an antiaircraft artillery school. She flew A-24s and A-25 Helldivers, towing targets for 90mm guns with live ammunition. She flew night searchlight target missions, radar deception missions dropping aluminum foil chaff, and low altitude missions for anti-aircraft tracking guns. Ruth said: *We did some cross-country flying and would follow the railroad to find our way at times. Every town had a water tower with a sextant on top of it so you knew what direction you were flying. But most of our flying was up and down range towing targets.*

After Camp Davis...
Ruth was transferred to Liberty Field, Georgia. She had 90 days of instruction and practice in piloting radio-controlled aircraft. After finishing

DAS Ruth Underwood
Florey – Later

that course she was sent to Biggs Army Air Field, Texas. At Biggs, she flew B-34s and B-26s in night searchlight missions and tracking missions for training anti-aircraft crews; radar tracking missions to train radio operators; radio-controlled target flying; low altitude night missions; and laying smoke screens. When the WASP were disbanded, Ruth married her long-time friend, a Skipper in the Navy.

Helen Wyatt Snapp

Helen was born May 1, 1918 in Washington, DC. She said: *I remember sitting on a curb on Pennsylvania Avenue, watching the Lindbergh parade*

pass by. I also followed newspaper accounts of Jacqueline Cochran and Amelia Earhart's accomplishments. Those probably were the things that influenced me most, so I dropped out of college and went to work to pay for flying lessons. When the Government's Civilian Pilot Training program started, I enrolled, worked, attended college, and took ground school classes in the evening.

Helen married her childhood "beau," Ira Snapp, and he was soon shipped overseas. Hearing about the flying training program for women,

HWS Helen Wyatt Snapp

she applied and was interviewed by Jacqueline Cochran. She was accepted and was off to Sweetwater, Texas. A little scared, this being her first real trip alone, she got off the train and found her way to a dingy, dark hotel. She soon met another WASP candidate and they became fast friends. The two were part of Class 43.4 that would train at Avenger Field.

Helen recalls: *Early in our training we did a lot of takeoffs and landings. It was important for us to be prepared for this most critical part of flying. As part of it we practiced landing in a crosswind. When you land in a crosswind you can't just land on the three wheels. Normally, you put down the wheel in the wind then set the other one down. Once that is learned you have confidence in about any windy condition. I loved to do the 'wheel landings.'*

I arrived at Camp Davis, a fresh recruit, right after Mabel Rawlinson crashed and died. It was not talked about much as Cochran didn't want it publicized. There was another accident when the pilot came in wheels up [on its belly]. The pilot was OK, but she was grounded and then taken to New York to face charges. Evidently, she was cleared because she flew the plane back to Camp Davis.

HWS Helen Wyatt Snapp – Later

Helen got involved in a new secret mission that was learning to fly radio-controlled PQ-8 drone planes. These were to replace target towing as a more accurate simulation of battle conditions for the antiaircraft gunners. This led to the development of the more sophisticated remote controlled planes of today.

After Camp Davis…

Helen transferred to Liberty Field, Georgia in March 1944 and for the rest of that year flew and trained PQ-8 and PQ-14 controllers and pilots.

After the WASP program ended in December, 1944, Helen went back to her home in Virginia. Her husband Ira Snapp, Jr. was still in the military in Europe. The 3rd Division C Company had served first in North Africa, Sicily, then France. Because of an injury he was assigned to the Quartermaster Corp and then helped supply troops in the Normandy Invasion. On his return in early 1945, he and Helen went on a road show with six officers to present displays and talk about Normandy as they promoted Savings Bonds

DAS Helen Wyatt
Snapp – 2005

all over the U.S. After this three month project, they returned home to Stanton, Virginia where they built a home and raised two children. Helen continued to fly as a hobby, but found it necessary to limit that, and eventually let her license lapse when vision problems developed.

The following biographies for Caro Bayley Bosca and Teresa James are provided since they shared many stories:

Additional Biographies

Caro Bayley Bosca and Teresa James were not at Camp Davis. But they both have much to contribute to the WASP story, so they have been included.

Caro Bayley Bosca

She was not a Camp Davis WASP, but I got to know Caro well, as she is the President of WASP and participates in all WASP events.

Caro Bayley was born March, 1922 in Springfield, Ohio. She had a yearning in her soul to fly and her father gave her tuition for a Civilian Pilot course as a graduation present from Saint Mary's Jr. College in Raleigh, North Carolina. After scraping through college, she found her flight ground school more to her liking, and particularly loved the flying. Her Civilian Pilot Training was accomplished at Springfield's Wittenberg University. She received her pilot's license in June of 1941. Then she took work filing flight plans at Patterson Field, now Wright-Patterson – AFB, to enable her get flight hours for a higher qualification.

She was the first in her class to master the loop. She managed to log 75 hours of flying by giving instruction in loops to other pilots. She worked her way into a job at the Traffic Desk and Message Center where all the pilot activity took place. While working there, she learned of the WASP program. All her previous work enabled her to qualify for WASP.

CBB Caro Bayley Bosca

At the end of May, 1943, she traveled to Sweetwater, Texas where she entered the WASP training program in Class 43.7 and received her silver wings at graduation in November of that year. She and nineteen other WASP were immediately sent to Mather Field in Sacramento, California for three months of B-25 Transition School, after which 10 of them reported to Biggs Field in El Paso, Texas where they became part of the Tow Target Squadron. She flew missions designed to test ground radar and antiaircraft capabilities.

CBB Caro's Aerobatics Plane

She flew the A-24, A-25, AT-11, AT-7, P-47, B-25 and B-26, for radar tracking, gassing, simulated strafing and searchlight missions. At that time, neighboring Fort Bliss was a large radar training center for ground troops. The WASP helped train these ground with similar missions. They stayed at Mather Field for nine months, until the WASP program was deactivated on December 20, 1944.

After deactivation, she wanted to keep flying, so along with some WASP alumni, she moved to Florida to work for her instructor rating. She learned aerobatic flying and got into competitive flying in air shows, flying Bristow's clip wing "Cub Cut Up." She also flew Ben Bradley's "Imp." It was during this time she found the first love of her life, the Curtis Pitts Special, a small, sleek, biplane called "Black Magic," the third he had built.

Caro took third place in acrobatics, competing with men, and became the Woman Aerobatics Champion. Her accomplishments led *Mademoiselle Magazine* to name her "Mademoiselle Woman of the Year in Aviation" in 1951 and she was also awarded the Bleriot medal for the altitude record of 30,203 feet for Class 2 aircraft in a Piper Super Cub with a 125 lycoming engine.

Teresa James

Teresa was born in Pittsburgh, Pennsylvania, in January, 1914. She was one of the "Originals" who brought some 10 years of flying experience to the WAFS and was one of the first women engaged in ferrying planes from factory to air base.

She began taking flying lessons in 1933 and earned her private pilot's license in October, 1934. Soon after, she was performing in air shows as a stunt pilot. Her signature stunt was a 26 turn spin. By 1941 she had an instructor pilot license as well as a commercial pilot license. She was also a volunteer for the Civil Air Patrol, helping them organize a new unit. In 1942 Teresa was a Civilian Pilot Training Program instructor in Pittsburgh, Pennsylvania and

DAS Teresa James Martin

had, by then, accumulated over 2000 logged hours.

James began her WAFS flying in September, 1942 and was based at New Castle Army Air Base in Wilmington, Delaware. She flew the first WAFS ferry mission in October of that year. One of her unique missions was to ferry a Fairchild PT-19 to California for use in a movie. She picked up the airplane in Hagarstown, Maryland and delivered it to the famous aviator Paul Mantz in Hollywood for use in "Ladies Courageous."

On September 20, 1944 Teresa was selected to fly the 10,000th P-47 that was built, from the Republic factory to its overseas embarkation point in Newark, New Jersey. By the time the WASP program ended in December, 1944, Teresa James was checked out in about 20 different types of military aircraft including the A-24, AT-6, AT-10, C-47, C-60, P-47 and P-51.

In 1950 Teresa was commissioned a major in the U.S. Air Force Reserves. She served until her retirement in 1976.

WASP Program Ends – Military Status Won

End of WASP

AS THE WAR'S end approached, large numbers of pilots were no longer needed. Male pilots had priority for available assignments, and many viewed the WASP as a threat. So the WASP program was disbanded in December, 1944. It should not be surprising that this was a terrible blow to WASP who found their real passion was flying, and the prospect of once again assuming the traditional roles expected for women was hard to take. They felt that they had made a big contribution to the war effort and now were being kicked out, virtually unacknowledged. Their thoughts were captured in the lines of a song:

> *They taught us how to fly,*
> *now they send us home to cry,*
> *'cause they don't want us anymore.*

The WASP program was a hybrid of war. The women were civilians, yet they were military in their behavior and discipline. While serving at an air base they were under that Commander's purview and could use military facilities, such as hospital care and officer's club. But, incredibly, at some locations they were expected to pay for their meals at the mess hall and their lodging. It is interesting to note that WASP received $150 a month while in training, and $250 a month once assigned. If a WASP was killed, she was not given a military burial, nor would the military pay for transportation of the body home. The families did not get any military assistance. Often, fellow WASP contributed their own money when it was needed. They received no military benefits until awarded military status over 30 years later.

So, in the end, the WASP program seemed destined to simply fade away with the women heading home unrecognized and virtually forgotten.

The Long Struggle for Recognition and Military Status

DAS WASP Life Magazine – 1943

By early 1944, U.S. air superiority had been achieved in Europe, and American pilots began to return home. Pilot training programs were shut down and civilian instructors who had served as non-enlisted now risked being drafted as foot soldiers. There was still a way around the draft, however, if they could assume the piloting jobs that the WASP were doing. There was a wave of popular support for this, and a rancorous campaign was launched against the WASP in the press and in Congress.

Supporters of the effort to win military status for the WASP were largely unheard and ignored. *Life Magazine*, for example, had long been supportive of the WASP. In 1943 they printed an issue with a WASP on the front cover and some six pages of photos promoting their accomplishments. But in 1944, with the tide shifting, *Life* and the media changed their focus; stories were written about America's desire to return to normal after the war, with women returning to traditional roles. An especially egregious attack on WASP and its leadership was waged by Drew Pearson who reported in his widely read "The Washington Merry-Go-Round" that Cochran, the "vivacious aviatrix," had seduced General Arnold into using a "back-door strategy" to get the WASP program approved; that unqualified women flew in the program and that WASP were inadequate pilots...among other vitriolic claims.

The tide of public opinion was being steered successfully against militarization of the WASP. And its supporters knew that if this bid for militarization failed, WASP would simply disappear without recognition and without proper support as veterans.

The opposition in Congress was spear-headed by Representative James Morrison of Louisiana who loaded his argument with personal attacks against General Hap Arnold.

In Congressional deliberations, Morrison read from an op-ed piece so it would be included as an "Extension of Remarks" in the *Congressional Record* of June, 1944. Morrison's remarks were:

> *The Evening Star*, one of the leading Washington papers, says WASP Program is "Wasted Money and Wasted Energy" and "Why spend $100,000 on the WASP Program? – Read what Miss Cassinni says." The latter piece alleged that the AAF was backing the WASP program because Cochran had seduced General Arnold:
>
> > In the last week the shapely pilot has seen her coveted commission coming closer and closer...One of the highest placed generals, it seems, gazed into her eyes, and since then has taken her cause celebre very much "to heart"... She's such an attractive composition of wind-blown bob, smiling eyes and outdoor skin, nobody blames him.
> >
> > It's whispered he's battling like a knight of olde, or

olde knight, for "the faire Cochran," So the announcement can be expected any day that Jackie's commission
has been approved, if the captivated general is victorious
in his tournaments.

Despite Hap Arnold's personal testimony and support from the
War Department, the bid for WASP militarization failed. Congress
recommended that all pilot training for women be stopped. They
also recommended that women pilots already in service continue
to fly, but without military status.

But for Jackie Cochran, there could be no compromise. She used
the very media that was denigrating her women and their program to turn the tide of opinion. She compiled an exhaustive report detailing the WASP accomplishments and released it to the
press. The report revealed that the WASP had flown over 60 million miles in every type of aircraft, and that their safety and performance records were comparable to male pilots. Cochran also gave
Hap Arnold an ultimatum – find a way to militarize the program
including pilot training under her command, or shut it down.

But Arnold could no longer fight Cochran's battle. He still had a
war to win and WASP were no longer a vital priority. In October,
1944 he announced the WASP would be deactivated on the 20th of
December. Nonetheless, in a moving speech to the final graduating
class, General Arnold acknowledged the WASP had exceeded all
expectations, even his own.

In the end, supporters' predictions largely came true. WASP and
their accomplishments went virtually unrecognized and they were
largely assimilated into traditional women's roles. The general
public has had little knowledge of the WASP contributions, and
histories rarely mention them.

WASP Recognition At Last

In 1976 the Air Force announced a major policy change; it planned to train its first women military pilots. This announcement generated a lot of media attention because it was claimed that women were going to pilot military planes for the first time.

Former WASP rose up to say: *Hold it…we were flying military planes in 1942 through 1944!* So new efforts to gain recognition of their WWII work began. And, of course, part of the fight was for them to be awarded military status and veterans' benefits.

A committee of former WASP was formed - the WASP Military Committee. The committee, with the assistance of Colonel Bruce Arnold, the son of General Hap Arnold, and Senator Barry Goldwater, who had served as a Ferrying Squadron pilot in WWII, introduced a militarization bill in the Senate. Representative Patsy Mink also submitted a bill to Congress. Neither made it through their respective Veterans' Affairs committees. In defense of the WASP, Colonel Bruce Arnold stated the solid intentions of his fa-

DP Militarization – Goldwater WASP 1977

TWU WASP Veteran Status – 1979 Wash.

ther, General Hap Arnold, to have WASP militarized, and he noted that the decision not to do so was a political one influenced by a powerful male civilian pilots' lobby. It was not the decision of the War Department.

WASP Ann Darr recollected in a *NY Times Magazine* article, May 7, 1995, that all the testimony from WASP and other support-ers seemed, in those early years, to fall on deaf ears. But when it turned out that one WASP's discharge papers were identical to those of a Congressional Committee member, objections crumbled: *I'll be danged*, the congressman drawled, *her discharge papers read just like mine!*

Finally, in 1977 Congress voted to recognize the WASP as vet-erans and award them veteran status from the United States Air Force. Being "militarized" meant they could at last receive an hon-orable military discharge and be considered veterans with all asso-ciated benefits. The bill was signed into law on Thanksgiving Eve,

1977, in the White House by President Jimmy Carter. Ironically, no WASP were present at the occasion to enjoy this historic moment. In 1984, each of the Women Airforce Service Pilots was awarded the Victory medal by President Ronald Reagan. Those who served on duty for more than a year during WWII also received the American Theater medal.

For the remaining WASP, the years since have been rich in remembrance and work, to bring their WASP story to the country. A National WASP WWII Museum has been established in Sweetwater, Texas, WASP displays are at various other museums across the nation including the Missiles and More Museum at Topsail Island, North Carolina. Commemorative events continue to be held at Sweetwater, Texas and other locations that attract WASP from the far reaches of the U.S. for reunions with their fellow pilots.

Source: *Clipped Wings* by Molly Merryman

Organizations and Activities

The Ninety-Nines

THIS ORGANIZATION WAS formed in 1929 and its charter members elected Amelia Earhart as their first president. The organization remains active to this day. The central mission, from its inception, was to combat the entrenched prejudices that still confront each woman who climbs into a cockpit. It has over 5500 members and continues to be dedicated to the advancement of women as pilots.

DAS Dawn Seymour, Ethel Finley, Caro Bosca,
Frances Sargent, Helen Snapp, Ruth Sleisher

DAS
Fran –
Fifinella
Sun 'n
Fun –
2005

DAS WASP Sun 'n Fun Display

DAS
WASP
Fly-In –
2005

The organization is very visible in its activities, having a number of events all over the U.S. each year. I attended one in April, 2005, a yearly "Sun 'n Fun Fly-In" at Lakeland, Florida. An acrobatic sky show kept me looking skyward and the display of all kinds of recreational airplanes was eye-opening. WASP participate in these events and have a similar enthusiasm to get together at their own reunions and Fly-Ins, most recently at Sweetwater, Texas.

Memorial Fly-In at Avenger Field, 2005

I attended an event at Sweetwater, Texas, at the airfield where the WASP were trained, a Memorial Fly-In. The women have a reunion at least every other year and with the creation of their Memorial Museum they will likely make this an annual event.

The main intent of this stellar affair was to introduce the beginnings of a National WASP WWII Museum there at Avenger Field. Forty WASP attended this gathering. It was exciting to see such

DAS WASP Memorial Fly-In – 2005

DAS Sun 'n Fun Bosca Display

DAS Fly-In WASP Flew This Plane

DAS Handprints at Fly-In – 2005

DAS WASP Imprints Fly-In

vitality in this group of 80 plus year old women. The women ceremoniously imprinted their hands into large slabs of concrete that will hold their images forever. A bronze statue of a WASP was on display along with many other remembrances. They had a forty-car parade in which the attending WASP were carried in a convertible from the airstrip to the museum celebration. They also had a fly-over of three planes, one missing from the usual formation of four, to honor those 38 WASP who gave their lives. It was an event I'll not soon forget.

National WASP WWII Museum at Avenger Field

At the Memorial Fly-In, 2005, an announcement was made about plans to build a permanent world-class museum there at Avenger Field. The mission of the museum:

> To educate, motivate and inspire generations-to-come with the history of the first women to fly America's military aircraft. This will be a permanent memorial – a lasting tribute and landmark to honor the WASP.

DAS WASP Interim Museum – 2005

The interim museum at Avenger houses displays and a prominent bronze statue of a WASP, beautifully sculpted by WASP Dot Swain Lewis. Its inscription:

> Dedicated to the unsung, who gave their time and their talents, toiling in the WASP WWII efforts without fame or fanfare.

DAS Scotty Bradley-Gough with
Sculpture by Dot Swain-Lewis Fly-In – 2005

Texas Woman's University – TWU, the National Archive for WASP

Texas Woman's University is located in Denton, Texas. The TWU Library contains the official WASP Archives and as such, provides an official source of WASP information.

WASP Stay in Touch

The WWII WASP of 1943 and 1944 continue to be a cohesive group. Their WASP organization keeps everyone informed of events, of what fellow WASP are doing, address changes, and deaths. The WASP organization is headed by Caro Bayley Bosca, President, and periodically distributes a professionally published WASP News to the membership.

Life-long bonds have kept individuals in touch, such as Frances Sargent and Helen Snapp. They remain close friends to this day and often attend WASP functions with many other flying friends. Helen said: *Our dwindling group from Liberty Field keeps in touch with a round-robin letter circulating now, for over 55 years!*

Author's Note

IN DECEMBER, 1994 Marion Hanrahan wrote in a WASP News article:

> Freddie Richardson phoned… We shared reminiscences about life at Houston and Camp Davis. We agreed that all the books written about the WASP adventure to date have failed to relate the simple joys, aggravations, and terrors we experienced during our unique contribution to the war effort. Perhaps it is time for someone to write the "real" Houston/ Camp Davis story.

After my first exposure to the WASP in the writing of *ECHOES of Topsail – Stories of the Island's Past*, my curiosity became infatuation with their story. The success of these young women at Camp Davis, piloting military aircraft in assignments that men thought females could never do, is little-known legend. Their story was too compelling to resist writing about it, and Hanrahan's note confirmed it for me.

My aim was to tell the story in WASP own words, to get a real sense of their experience. Imagine the thrill of finding those still living and able to tell their story. I was impressed as the acronyms and airplane codes rolled off their tongues even after all these years. Finding Betty Deuser Budde's letters at Texas Woman's University was the clincher for how to get their insights into that experience. Betty generously allowed me to include her letters with the caution that she was a young homesick girl when writing them.

It is my hope that Camp Davis WASP agree that my book captures the *real* story.

Appendix

WASP Bronze Sculptures

WASP Memorials have been sculpted by two WASP and have found homes in various places across the U. S. They are in long-life bronze and are approximate life sized for a petite WASP. Dot Swain Lewis and Pfeifer Estes are the sculptors.

Locations:

Texas State Technical College at Avenger Field. Sweetwater, Texas. Swain-Lewis

Texas Woman's University Library. Denton, Texas. Pfeifer Estes

U. S. Air Force Museum. Wright-Patterson AFB. Dayton, Ohio. Swain-Lewis

Confederate Air Force Headquarters. Midland, Texas. Swain-Lewis.

Colorado Air Force Academy. Colorado Springs, Colorado. Swain-Lewis

National WASP WWII Museum. Sweetwater, Texas. Swain-Lewis

The Highground Veteran's Memorial Park. Neillsville, Wisconsin. Swain-Lewis

Air Force Bases Where Wasp Served

1st AF:

Camp Davis, North Carolina; Liberty Field [Camp Stewart], Georgia; Otis, Massachusetts.

2nd AF:

Alamagordo, New Mexico; Casper, Wyoming; Clovis, New Mexico; Dalhart, Texas; Dyersburg, Tennessee; Fort Sumner, New Mexico; Gowen, Idaho; Grand Island, Nebraska; Great Bend, Kansas; Peterson, Colorado; Pocatello, Idaho; Pratt, Kansas; Pueblo, Colorado; Roswell, New Mexico; Smoky Hill, Kansas; Strother, Kansas; Walker, Kansas.

3rd AF:

Biggs, Texas; Deming, New Mexico.

4th AF:

Half Moon Bay Flight Strip, California; Hamilton, California; March, California; Salinas, California.

WASP Program
Requirements & Conclusions

Objectives of the WASP Program stated by the Commanding General of the Army Air forces:

1. To see if women could serve as military pilots and if so, to form the nucleus of an organization that could be rapidly expanded;

2. To release male pilots from non-for combat;

3. To decrease the Air Forces' total demands on the cream of the manpower pool.

Requirements for the original ferrying group were fixed by the Air Transport Command:

1. Age limit – 21 to 35 inclusive

2. High school education

3. Commercial pilot license with 200 hp rating

4. Not less than 500 hours of logged and certified time

5. American citizenship

6. Cross-country flying experience

These requirements were intended for the first ferrying group and required minimal training to be qualified on military aircraft.

The requirements were modified to less rigorous requirements to qualify more women for entry into the Avenger six month training program.

1. Age – 21 to 35 inclusive

2. High school education or equivalent

3. Minimum height 60 inches

4. 200 hours flying time

5. Medical examination by an Army flight surgeon

6. American citizenship

7. Personal interview with an authorized recruiting officer

Within a few months, the requirements were modified further to a minimum age of $18^1/_2$ years and a logged flight time of 35 hours. (Civilian Cub license level)

Conclusions of Jacqueline Cochran are paraphrased here:

1. Women of equivalent physical attributes can be trained as quickly as men and fly all types of planes safely and efficiently.

2. The best women pilots are closer to the age $18^1/_2$ limit.

3. WASP have effectively released male pilots for other duties.

4. Physiology peculiar to women is not a handicap to flying or dependable performance of duty.

5. The psychological, aptitude and other tests for male pilots have the same usefulness for women pilots.

6. The flying safety record of women pilots approximates that of male pilots.

7. Women pilots have as much stamina and endurance. Women can safely fly as many hours in a month as male pilots.

8. Even limiting the selection of women pilots to the physical characteristics mentioned above, an effective woman's air force of many thousands of dependable pilots could be built up, if needed.

Source: War Department Air Force Documents

World War II
Aircraft Production

World War II Aircraft Production by Country and Year							
Country	1939	1940	1941	1942	1943	1944	1945
UK	7,940	15,049	20,094	23,672	26,263	26,461	12,070
US	2,141	6,086	19,433	47,836	85,898	96,318	46,001
USSR	10,382	10,565	15,735	25,436	34,900	40,300	20,900
Germany	8,295	10,826	12,401	15,409	24,807	40,593	7,540
Japan	4,467	4,768	5,088	8,861	16,693	28,180	8,263

Above and Beyond: Total Program
1074 – 38 WASP Lost Their Lives

T – Trainee   A – Active Duty

NAME	STATUS	CLASS	DATE	PLANE	PLACE
*Champlin, Jane	T*	43-4	3 Jun 43	BT-15	Westbrook, TX
Clarke, Susan	A*	44-2	4 Jul 44	BT-15	Columbia, SC
Davis, Margie L.	T	44-9	16 Oct 44	AT-6	Walnut, MS
Dussaq, Katherine	A	44-1	26 Nov 44	AT-8	New Carlisle, OH
Edwards, Marjorie	T	44-6	13 Jun 44	AT-8	Nr Childress, TX
Erickson, Elizabeth	T	44-6	16 Apr 44	PT-17	Nr Sweetwater, TX
*Fort, Cornella	A	WAFS	21 Mar 43	BT-13	Merkel, TX
Grimes, Frances	A	43-3	27 Mar 44	A-24	Otis Fld, MA
*Hartson, Mary	A	43-5	14 Aug 44	BT-13	Nr Perrin, TX
Howson, Mary	T	44-4	16 Apr 44	AT-6	Nr Sweetwater, TX
Keene, Edith	A	44-1	25 Apr 44	BT-13	Nr Mission, TX
Lawrence, Kathryn	T	43-8	3 Aug 43	PT-19	Nr Sweetwater, TX
*Lee, Hazel Ying	A	43-4	23 Nov 44	P-63	Great Falls, MT
*Loop, Paula	A	43-2	7 Jul 44	BT-15	Medford, OR
*Lovejoy, Alice	A	43-5	13 Sep 44	AT-6	Brownsville, TX
McDonald, Loa O.	A	44-3	21 Jun 44	A-24	Biggs AFB, TX
Martin, Peggy	A	44-4	3 Oct 44	BT-13	Marana, AZ
*McPlatt, Virginia	A	43-2	5 Oct 43	BT-13	Ontario, CA
Moses, Beverly	A	44-5	18 Jul 44	AT-11	Nr Las Vegas, NV
*Nichols, Dorothy	A	43-2	11 Jun 44	P-39	Bismarck, ND
Norbock, Jeanne	A	44-3	16 Oct 44	BT-13	Shaw Fld, SC
Oldenburg, Margaret	T	43-4	7 Mar 43	PT-19	Nr Houston, TX
*Rawlinson, Mabel	A	43-3	23 Aug 43	A-24	Camp Davis, NC
Roberts, Gleanna	T	44-9	20 Jun 44	PT-17	Lorraine, TX
Robinson, (Michell) Marie	A	44-2	2 Oct 44	B-25	Victorville, CA
Scott, Bettie Mae	A	44-3	8 Jul 44	BT-13	Waco, TX
Scott, Dorothy	A	WAFS	3 Dec 43	BC-1	Palm Springs, CA
Soip, Margaret	T	43-5	30 Aug 43	UC-78	Nr Big Spring, TX
Soverson, Helen	T	43-5	30 Aug 43	UC-78	Nr Big Spring, TX
Sharon, Ethel Marie	A	43-4	10 Apr 44	B-25	Tecumseh, NB
*Sharp, Evelyn	A	WAFS	3 Apr 44	P-38	New Cumberland, PA
*Tompkins (Silver) Gertrude	A	43-7	16 Oct 44	P-51	Betwn Long Beach and Palm Springs, CA
Stino, Betty	T	44-2	25 Feb 44	AT-6	Nr Quartzite, AZ
Toovs, Marion	A	43-8	18 Feb 44	BT-13	San Jose, CA
Trebing, Mary	A	43-4	5 Oct 43	PT-17	Nr Norman, OK
Webster, Mary	A	44-8	9 Dec 44	BT-15	Claremore, OK
Wolz, Bonnie Jean	4A	43-6	29 Jun 44	BT-13	Randado, TX
Wood, Betty Taylor	A	43-4	9 Sep 43	A-24	Camp Davis, NC

Source: Andy Hailey's Web Pages
www-women-pilots.org/WASP_KIA/38KIA.html

Drawing of Camp Davis

Runway (1)

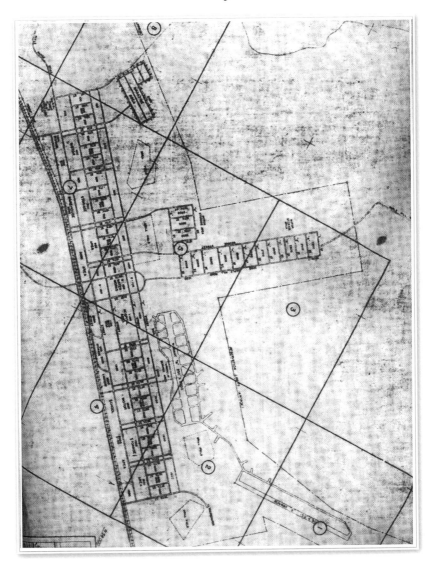

Some Of The Aircraft Flown By Wasp

AAF NUMS	PURPOSE/USE	# ENGINES / HP	BUILT BY	PLANE NAME
L-4	Cargo; Spotter	1 / 65	Piper	Grasshopper
A-24	Dive Bomber; Tow Target	1 / 1200	Douglas	Dauntless
A-25	Dive Bomber; Tow Target	1 / 1750	Curtis	Helldiver
AT-6	Advanced Trainer	2 / 600	North American	Texan
AT-7	Bombardier; Gunner Trainer	2 / 450	Beechcraft	Kansan
AT-11	Bombardier; Gunner Trainer	2 / 450	Beechcraft	Kansan
AT-17	Liaison; Cargo	2 / 245	Cessna	Bamboo Bomber
B-17	Heavy Bomber	4 / 1200	Boeing	Flying Fortress
B-29	Heavy Bomber	4 / 2200	Boeing	Superfortress
BT-13	Basic Trainer	1 / 450	Vultee	Valiant; Vibrator
BT-15	Basic Trainer	1 / 450	Vultee	Valiant; Vibrator
P-38	Pursuit	2 / 1425	Lockheed	Lightning
P-47	Fighter; Bomber Escort	1 / 2800	Republic	Thunderbolt; Jug
P-51	Fighter; Bomber Escort	1 / 1380	North American	Mustang
PT-13	Primary Trainer	1 / 220	Stearman	Kaydet
PQ-8	Drone Target	1 / 125	Culver	Kaydet
PQ-14	Drone Target	1 / 150	Culver	No Name

Pilot Checklist

PILOT'S CHECK LIST

BC-1, BC-1A, AT-6, AT-6A, AT-6B, AT-6C, SNJ-3 and -4
R 1340-AN-1 Engine

BEFORE STARTING ENGINES

1. Check Form one.
2. Fasten Safety Belt.
3. Set parking brakes.
4. UNLOCK surface controls—Check operation.
5. Fuel selector—reserve—check for quantity.
6. Prop. HIGH PITCH.
7. Mixture FULL RICH.
8. Throttle (800-900 R.P.M.)
9. Carb. heat COLD.
10. Prime 4 to 6 strokes when cold.
11. Generator main line switches ON.
12. Battery switch ON (Not applicable BC-1.)
13. Ignition switch BOTH ON—energize—engage.

DURING WARM UP

1. Oil Pressure up, shift prop. to LOW PITCH. Warm up at 1,000 R.P.M.
2. Check magnetos at 29 in. hg.
3. Check operation of prop control-flaps-elevator and rudder trim-generator.
4. Check radio, clock and altimeter.

BEFORE TAKE OFF

1. Prop INCREASE R.P.M., LOW PITCH.
2. Mixture RICH.
3. Carb. heat COLD.
4. Oil temp. 40 degrees C. minimum, 95 degrees C. maximum.
5. Cyl. temp. 160 degrees C. minimum, 260 degrees C. maximum.
6. Take off 36 in. Hg, 2250 R.P.M.

DURING FLIGHT

1. Landing gear UP.
2. Mixture. When operating at high powers below 5000 ft. altitude, leave mixture control in FULL RICH. For all other conditions, use the following FUEL-AIR ratios are desired. Do not exceed allowable cylinder head temperature when leaning out:

POWER	R.P.M.	MP in Hg.	F-A
Climb and high speed	2200	32.5	.089
Cruising-Maximum	1925	29.0	.073
Cruising desired	1850	26.0	.072
Diving-maximum	2040	20.0	.089

BEFORE LANDING

1. Landing gear DOWN.
2. Propeller 1925 R.P.M.
3. Mixture RICH.
4. Fuel selector on RESERVE.
5. Flaps are required (Below 120 M.P.H.)
6. CAGE gyro and flight indicator.

AFTER LANDING

1. Flaps UP.
2. Propeller HIGH PITCH.
3. Oil dilution as necessary.
4. Mixture IDLE CUT OFF.
5. SET brakes and LOCK controls.
6. All electrical switches OFF.

A pilot's check list for a AT-6 Texan. The AT-6 was the advanced trainer used in the final phase of the WASP training at Avenger Field, Sweetwater, Texas.

Frances Rohrer –
A Flight Record of 23 Days

Individual Flight Record form.

DAY	AIRCRAFT TYPE, MODEL & SERIES	NO. LANDINGS	FLYING INST. (INCL. IN 1ST PIL. TIME) S	COMMD. PILOT C CA	CO-PILOT CP	QUALI-FIED PILOT DUAL QD	FIRST PILOT DAY P	FIRST PILOT NIGHT P N OR NI	NON-PILOT I	OTHER ARMS & SERVICES	OTHER CREW & PASS GR	INSTR.MENT I	NIGHT N	INSTRU-MENT TRAINER	PILOT NON-MIL AIRCRAFT OVER 400 H.P.	UNDER 400 H.P.
	19	20	21	22	23	24	25	26	27	28	29	30	31	32	33	34	35	36
4	AT-11	1					1:30									
4	AT-11				1:30											
5	UC-78	4					1:10									
5	UC-78	4			:20											
7	L-5	2					1:00									
11	AT-11	6					:40									
11	AT-11	6						:40								
11	L-5	1					2:05									
12	UC-78	1					1:25									
12	UC-78				1:25											
13	RA-25-A	4					3:50									
13	R-37	1			1:40											
14	UC-78	2			1:40											
14	UC-78	2					1:45									
17	UC-78	6						1:00								
17	UC-78	3					:30							:30		
17	UC-78	2					1:15									
17	UC-78	2			1:15											
17	AT-11	2						1:00								
17	AT-11	2					:35									
18	Link														1:00	
18	RA-25-A	2					3:05									
19	AT-11	8					:35	:40								
20	Link														1:20	
20	RB-34A	1			2:25											
18	UC-78	1			:55								:55		
22	UC-78	1						1:40								
23	UC-78	1			1:55											
23	AT-11	1			1:55								1:55		
21	RA-25-A	1					3:05									

WASP Could Participate
in Officer Training

THE ANTIAIRCRAFT ARTILLERY SCHOOL
Camp Davis, North Carolina

......February 11, 1944........

CERTIFICATE OF COMPLETION OF
AIR OFFICERS COURSE

I Certify that .... W.A.S.P., Francis N. Rohrer, A.A.F. ....

satisfactorily completed a course of instruction held at THE ANTIAIRCRAFT ARTILLERY SCHOOL

as listed above during the period....... February 7, 1944 ....,

to.............................. February 11, 1944 ....

For the COMMANDANT:

Chandler S. Kimball

CHANDLER S. KIMBALL,
1st Lt. C.A.C.
Asst. Registrar.

Recorded on page..............
Volume I, Record of
Diplomas and Certificates.

Frances Rohrer Sargent–

Honored as Tailhooker

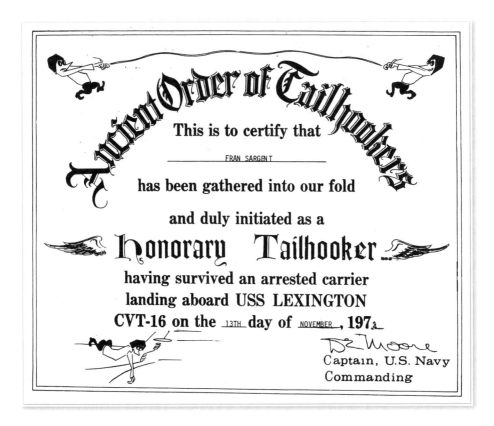

This is to certify that

FRAN SARGENT

has been gathered into our fold

and duly initiated as a

Honorary Tailhooker

having survived an arrested carrier
landing aboard USS LEXINGTON
CVT-16 on the 13TH day of NOVEMBER, 1973

Captain, U.S. Navy
Commanding

Commanding General
H.H. Arnold Letter

HEADQUARTERS, ARMY AIR FORCES
WASHINGTON

YOUNG PEOPLE OF AMERICA:

The future of American aviation rests with you, the youth of America. All of us who had to do with the building of the great Army Air Forces that cleared its enemies from the sky have known for years that the domain of the air is preeminently for the young.

Never was aviation's need for healthy, alert youth made clearer than during the past war. Then the need became the need of our Country for if we were to be victorious we had to have forces in the air superior to anything the enemy could send up. The need was for superiority in planes and equipment but above all superiority in man.

We got that superiority - in planes and equipment, and in man. From farms and from cities, from schools and from jobs came our young men and young women, to plan and build and fly and maintain the mighty air forces that brought us victory. The victory that justified the faith we all had in American youth and air power.

Now we have turned into a time of peace, which I hope will be time without end. The rewards of peace are ever greater than the rewards of war. Peacetime aviation lies ahead, promising a rich harvest of opportunity and satisfying experience for air-minded youth and providing also the training ground, the know-how and experience for time of emergency.

For her future security America needs a thriving peacetime aviation industry and a great commercial aviation. She needs intense public interest and support of aviation. She needs thinking and planning and scientific research. She needs healthy young men and women, healthy mentally, spiritually and physically. She needs all these things to support and sustain her military air forces.

Once again America expects to find her strength in her youth. She looks to you for the best pilots on earth, for the best navigators, the best radio operators, the best mechanics, the best radar experts, the best designers, the best scientists, the best of every person who helps make up the big family of the air.

America puts her faith in you. Tomorrow the air will be yours. I know you will treat your heritage wisely and well.

H.H. ARNOLD,
Commanding General, Army Air Forces

Bibliography

Books about WASP

Backus, Jean L. *Amelia*. Boston, Massachusetts: Beacon Press, 1982.

Carl, Ann B. *A WASP Among Eagles: Woman Military Test Pilot in World War II*. Washington, DC: The Smithsonian Institution, 1999.

Cole, Jean Hascall. *Women Pilots of World War II*. Salt Lake City, Utah: University of Utah Press, 1992.

Dailey, Janet. *Silver Wings, Santiago Blue*. New York, New York: Poseidon Press, 1984.

Granger, Byrd Howell. *On Final Approach: The Women Airforce Service Pilots of WWII*. Scottsdale, Arizona: Falconer Publishing Company, 1991.

Hodgson, Marion Stegeman. *Winning My Wings*. Albany, Texas: Bright Sky Press, 2004.

Keil, Sally Van Wagenen. *Those Wonderful Women in Their Flying Machines: The Unknown Heroines of World War II*. Rhinebeck, New York: Four Directions Press, 1979.

Langley, Wanda. *Flying Higher: The Women Airforce Service Pilots of*

World War II. North Haven, Connecticut: Linnet Book, 2002.

Merryman, Molly. *Clipped Wings: The Rise and Fall of the Women Airforce Service Pilots (WASPs) of World War II.* New York, New York: New York University Press, 1998.

Nathan, Amy. *Yankee Doodle Gals: Women Pilots of World War II.* Washington, DC: National Geographic Society, 2001.

Noggle, Anne. *For God, Country, and the Thrill of It: Women Airforce Service Pilots in World War II.* College Station, Texas: Texas A & M University Press, 1990.

Rickman, Sarah Byrn. *The Originals: The Women's Auxiliary Ferrying Squadron of World War II.* Sarasota, Florida: Disc-Us Books, Inc., 2001.

Roberts, Marjorie H. *Wingtip to Wingtip: 8 WASPs.* Marjorie H. Roberts, 2000.

Simbeck, Rob. *Daughter of the Air: The Brief Soaring Life of Cornelia Fort.* New York, New York: Grove Press, 1999.

Stallman, David A. *ECHOES of Topsail - Stories of the Island's Past.* Wilmington, NC: Echoes Press, 2004.

Turner, Betty Stagg. *Out of the Blue and Into History.* Arlington Heights, Illinois: Aviatrix Publishing, Inc., 2001.

Tyndall, Clifford. *Greetings from Camp Davis: The History of a WWII Army Base.* Chapel Hill, North Carolina: Chapel Hill Press, 2006.

Wood, Winifred. *We Were WASPS.* Coral Gables, Florida: Glade House Publishers, 1945.

Articles

Bollow, John. "Remembering the WASPS." The Saturday Evening Post, May/June, 1995.

Darr, Ann. "The Women Who Flew – But Kept Silent." The New York Times Magazine, May 7, 1995.

Hager, Alice Rogers. "Women As Service Pilots." Skyways Magazine, February, 1944.

McGaha, Laura. "Laurine Nielsen Transcribed Diary, 1943." The Woman's Collection, Texas Woman's University, 2004.

Salazar, Felicia. "Betty Deuser Budde Letters, 1943-1944." The Woman's Collection Texas Woman's University, 2004.

Stallman, David A. "A History of Camp Davis." Hampstead Services, 1990.

Websites

Hailey, C. Andy. http://wwii.women-pilots.org

National WASP WWII Museum. www.avengerfield.org

Stallman, David A. http://members.aol.com/StallmanD/

Texas Woman's University. www.TWU.edu/wasp/

WASP on the Web. www.wasp-wwii.org/wasp/

Wings Across America. www.wasp-wwii.org/wings/

WWII Searchlights. www.skylighters.org/intrduction/index.html

Photo Credits

ACT   Alta Corbett Thomas

BDB   Betty Deuser Budde

CAH   C. Andy Hailey's Web Pages – Kid of WASP

CBB   Caro Bayley Bosca

DAS   David A. Stallman Collection

DP   Deanie Parrish

GD   Gustave Dubbs

JD   Jim DeGuiseppi

FRS   Frances Rohrer Sargent

HWS   Helen Wyatt Snapp Collection

JAM   John A. McKeown

JHU   John Hopkins University Applied Physics Laboratory

JR   Justin Raphael

MLV   Marty Lawson Volkomener

MMM   Missiles and More Museum

TWU   The Woman's Collection, Texas Woman's University

WAA   Wings Across America

Cover Picture – *Lady Dauntless,*
         an original painting by Priscilla Messner-Patterson

Index

D

DeGuiseppi, Jim   62, 233

Deuser, Betty. *See* Budde, Betty Deuser

Dougherty, Dora. *See* McKeown, Dora Dougherty Strother

Drones. *See* Radio-Controlled Drones

Dubbs, Gus. *See* Dubbs, Gustave

Dubbs, Gustave   64, 65, 233

Dyer, Elsie. *See* Monaco, Elsie Dyer

E

Earhart, Amelia   XI, 11, 157, 158, 174, 176, 190, 205

Ellington, June. *See* Petto, June Ellington

El Paso   119, 120, 121, 122, 152, 154, 156, 163, 164, 168, 170, 177, 193

F

Fenton, Isabel. *See* Stinson, Isabel Fenton

Fifinella   37, 38, 206

Florey, Ruth Underwood   63, 73, 105, 159, 188, 189, 190

Fort, Cornelia   125, 230

Fort Fisher   51, 60, 61, 62, 63, 65

G

Giles, Major General Barnell   47, 145, 172

Goldwater, Barry   201

Grant, Mary Hines   72, 133

Greene, Elizabeth   72

Grimes, Frances   72, 108

H

Hailey, Lois Brooks   15, 17, 25, 71, 75, 78, 81, 82, 83, 84, 95, 107, 108, 120, 155, 157, 159, 162, 163, 164, 166, 167, 168, 169, 177

Hanrahan, Marion   72, 93, 102, 132, 159, 174, 175, 213

Harkness, Nancy. *See* Love, Nancy Harkness

Harte, Elin   72, 108

Hines, Mary. *See* Grant, Mary Hines

Hinman, Second Lieutenant   107

Holben, Margery Moore   72

Hollingsworth, Lois. *See* Ziler, Lois Hollingsworth

M

N

O

P

Stephenson, Colonel Lovick   XVIII, 48, 49, 93, 106
Stinson, Isabel Fenton   72, 111, 112
Stortz, Caryl Jones   72
Strother, Dora. *See* McKeown, Dora Dougherty Strother
Sun 'n Fun   206, 207, 208
Sweetwater. *See* Avenger Field

T

Taylor, Betty. *See* Wood, Betty Taylor
TB-26   154
Texas   IX, XVII, 4, 15, 16, 17, 19, 21, 111, 119, 120, 122, 152, 155, 156, 161,
     163, 166, 167, 168, 169, 170, 171, 176, 177, 179, 182, 184, 186, 188,
     189, 190, 193, 203, 207, 210, 213, 215, 216, 229, 230, 231, 233
Texas Woman's University   IX, 122, 210, 213, 215, 231, 233
Thackara, Shirley Ingalls   72, 94, 108
Thomas, Alta Corbett   71, 159, 164, 165, 233
Thompson, Viola. *See* Mason, Viola Thompson
Tibbets, Paul W.   142, 143, 144, 145, 172, 173, 178
Titland, Kathleen Kelly   72
Toner, Mildred. *See* Chapin, Mildred Toner
Topsail Island   47, 203
Tow Target   48, 86, 128, 132, 161, 163, 165, 168, 178, 186, 188, 193, 222
Trask, Bertha Link   72, 94, 108

U

UC-78   116, 118, 119, 122, 165, 186, 220
Underwood, Ruth. *See* Florey, Ruth Underwood

V

Vanderpoel, Lila Chapman   71, 95, 108, 133
Volkomener, Martha Lawson   28, 72, 159, 179, 180, 181, 233

W

Ware, Emma Coulter   72, 95, 108, 120, 156, 157, 159, 166, 167, 169, 177
Washington. *See* Washington, DC
Washington, DC   XV, 12, 19, 41, 48, 75, 76, 78, 79, 109, 112, 162, 163, 166,
     169, 176, 184, 186, 190, 199, 229, 230
Wichita   109, 151, 152
Widget   156, 157